T0064836

ALIENS *AND THE* UNEXPLAINED

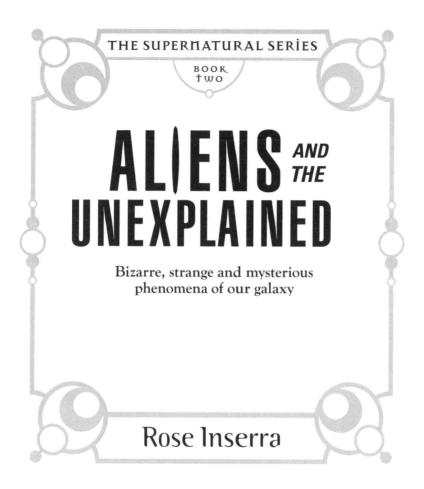

THE SUPERNATURAL SERIES

BOOK
TWO

ALIENS *AND THE* UNEXPLAINED

Bizarre, strange and mysterious
phenomena of our galaxy

Rose Inserra

ROCKPOOL
PUBLISHING

A Rockpool book
PO Box 252
Summer Hill
NSW 2130
Australia
www.rockpoolpublishing.com.au
http://www.facebook.com/RockpoolPublishing

First published in 2016
Text Copyright © Rose Inserra 2016

Images cover: Getty Images; page 6: 'The Great Martian God' (PaleoContact.com); page 7: Aboriginal Wandjinas (Graeme Churchard); page 16: Sumerian tablet, The Adda Seal (British Museum); page 21: 'Akhenaten' (Wikipedia/Gerard Ducher); page 33: 'Alien Landing Strip Teotihuacan' (Wikipedia); pages 34 & 35: 'Golden Aircraft' (TheAncientAliens.com); page 36: 'Ancient Pilots' (rijksmuseumamsterdam.blogspot.com); page 37: Artist unknown, *The Crucifixion* (Blago Fund Archives); page 38: Domenico Ghirlandaio, *The Madonna with Saint Giovannino*; page 39: Aert De Gelder, *The Baptism of Christ*; page 44: 'UFO' (Shutterstock); page 59: front page, Roswell Daily Record, 8 July 1947; page 75: 'The Nazi Bell' (Zusurs); page 100: 'The Greys' (Shutterstock); page 102: 'The Nordics' (Shutterstock); page 107: 'Sirian Landscape' (Shutterstock); page 122: Crop circles; page 124: Bermuda Triangle; page 131: 'Crystal Skull' (Rafal Chalgasiewicz); page 140: 'Face on Mars'; page 144: Stonehenge

The publisher and author have made every effort to contact copyright holders. If any copyright holder has been omitted, please contact us.

National Library of Australia Cataloguing-in-Publication entry
Inserra, Rose, 1958- author.

Aliens and the unexplained : bizarre, strange and mysterious
        phenomena of our galaxy / Rose Inserra.

9781925017489 (hardback)

Supernatural series ; Book Two.
Unidentified flying objects--Anecdotes.
        Extraterrestrial beings--Anecdotes.
        Human-alien encounters--Anecdotes.
        Curiosities and wonders.

001.942

Edited by Katie Evans
Cover and internal design by Jessica Le, Rockpool Publishing
Typesetting by Graeme Jones
Printed and bound in China

10 9 8 7 6 5 4 3 2

Contents

Introduction

---◦◦◯◦◦---

Are we alone on this vast planetary playground? Or are
there other players out there?

It's impossible for us to imagine the immensity of our
galaxy, the Milky Way, which measures up to 120,000
light years across space and contains about 400 billion stars.
It's said that about half of these stars include at least one
planet within their orbit. Thousands of these planets must
surely host ideal conditions to support life – civilisations
other than our own.

But we are still learning about our own galaxy. Recent
discoveries in astronomy and quantum physics have made
us sit up and pay attention. In a groundbreaking discovery,
NASA has confirmed evidence that liquid water flows
intermittently on Mars. This has been a surprise to us, since
we have always thought of Mars as arid and not being able
to support life.

What's more, a new, ninth planet, has been discovered! A
celestial body nearly the size of Neptune lurks beyond Pluto.
It is yet to be seen by the human eye, as it orbits the sun
once in every 15,000 years.

By far what's excited the scientific community the most is the fact that scientists have finally witnessed the warping of space-time that is generated by the collision of two black holes more than a billion light years from Earth. This is known as Einstein's 'gravitational waves'. As a result of this discovery, we will get a better understanding of how life on Earth first began and even the beginnings of the universe itself.

How far we've come! But there is the question of whether we can ever find out if we are alone. Is there intelligent alien life in the galaxy and beyond, and, if so, what are the chances that aliens have visited Earth? It seems our ancestors witnessed visits from 'the gods', who came down in 'chariots of fire', and 'angels'.

How do we reconcile the inexplicable rise and fall of major civilisations and their superior knowledge? Was it alien-guided?

Forensic investigations have also made huge progress – and not a minute too soon. With new archaeological sites being discovered and strange skulls with non-identifiable human DNA strands, it's going to be a wild ride as we track down our ancestry with more determination than ever before.

When you think of aliens, most people think of Roswell and the flying saucer crash. Many UFOlogists claim that Area 51, a US Air Force facility in Nevada, holds the remains of the alleged crash in 1947, including alien bodies, and has been covered up by the US government.

Recently, in an interview reported in January 2016, Hillary Clinton promised to disclose everything about the Roswell and UFO incident if she gets to the White House.

Many UFO sightings have been splashed across newspapers and witnessed by crowds in major cities. But somehow the official response from government agencies has been to discredit the people, play it down and make it go away. Only now, with social media and superior video cams and binoculars, apps and other high-tech support, it has never been easier to film, upload and share those strange lights in the sky.

Whether one is a believer in UFOs or not, there simply cannot be so many weather balloons, planes or satellites in the sky as are being reported.

Back to the age-old question – *Are we alone?*

It seems we have never been closer to finding out.

Part One

Our Planet, Our Galaxy

—o—o—O—o—o—

'If we want to set out on the arduous search for the truth, we must all summon up the courage to leave the lines along which we have thought until now and as the first step begin to doubt everything that we previously accepted as correct and true. Can we still afford to close our eyes and stop up our ears because new ideas are supposed to be heretical and absurd?'

Erich von Däniken, Chariots of The Gods

If ancient aliens did indeed visit Earth in prehistoric times they would have been regarded as 'gods' just as we would be considered god-like creatures if we were to go back in time with our modern aircraft. Our aeroplanes in their eyes would probably look like giant metal birds, spitting fire and making the earth shake. What power we would have. We couldn't possibly be human – we would have to be gods. Gods from the heavens. If this scenario was playing in a remote tribe in the highlands of New Guinea or the Amazon today, this may still be the reaction. Try to explain lasers and space suits, rovers and drones, let alone the spacecraft itself.

Theorists of ancient alien life believe that something like this did happen to our ancestors, and they passed down their observations the best way they knew how: stories and pictures.

Petroglyphs found on cave and mountain walls tell us the same visual story: strange beings or 'gods' had visited primitive man.

The Great Martian God

In the Sahara desert, a strange figure painted on the wall of a cave, identified as the 'Great Martian God', is located in the Tassili mountains in North Africa. It is dated around 6000 BCE.

The Australian Aboriginal rock art of the Wandjinas

This is one of the most intriguing examples of Aboriginal cave art dating back 60,000 years. It is found in the Kimberley region, Australia. It features the representation of the legend of the Wandjinas, the supreme spirit beings and creators of land and sea and Earth's inhabitants. They were known as 'sky beings' or 'spirits from the clouds', who came down from the Milky Way. The most striking features are the white faces, the absence of a mouth, large black eyes, and a head surrounded by a halo or some type of helmet. Did extra-terrestrial beings come into direct contact with a remote primitive tribe tens of thousands of years ago? What else could these beings be?

The Strange Space Traveller

A strange suited figure found in Kiev dates back to 4000 BCE. A helmet, a necessity for human space explorers, would come in handy for an alien space traveller.

Were the Gods Extra-terrestrials?

The Mayan *Popol Vuh*, also known as the Council Book, contains the myths and genealogy of rulers of the Quiche kingdom of Guatemala. Alien life existed in South America during the early 15th century.

> 'Men came from the stars, knowing everything, and they examined the four corners of the sky and the Earth's round surface.'

The Mayan *Chilam Balaam* texts of Mexico also state:

> 'Beings descended from the sky in flying vessels …
> white men in flying rings, who can touch the sky.'

Could extra-terrestrials with superior knowledge of science and engineering have landed on Earth thousands of years ago or more, sharing their knowledge with early civilisations? Is this how the Mayans of Mexico, the Sumerians of Mesopotamia (now Southern Iraq) and the Egyptians, especially, got their advanced knowledge in astronomy, mathematics and science?

Ancient astronaut theorist and author of *Chariots of the Gods*, Erich von Däniken claimed that advanced knowledge, technologies and religions of our ancient civilisations were given to them by space travellers, who were considered gods by our early ancestors.

Ancient artworks throughout the world depict what appear to be astronauts, spaceships, winged creatures with machines that came from 'heaven', extra-terrestrials that looked like men or were hybrids, and complex technologies.

Why Did Aliens Come Here?

Have you ever wondered how techologically advanced some ancient civilisations were for their time? From the main advanced civilisations there is a resounding yes. Ancient Sumerian tablets describe an alien race known as the *Anunnaki,* who came to Earth to mine for gold. Egyptian hieroglyphs depict hybrid creatures that were part man, part animal. Was it a form of genetic engineering in which hybrids were created from humans and aliens? Mysterious crop circles, and landing tracks and unexplained pyramid landing pads are only some clues that there are continuous visits from alien life from these locations.

Strange evidence in many ancient cultures suggests that aliens came to Earth to explore, excavate raw materials such as gold, experiment on human beings, and simply to conquer. Creation stories also support the alien god theory.

The ancient Sumerian civilisation was flourishing about 4500 BCE and existed in what was once Mesopotamia (modern day Iraq). Their sophistication seemed to come out of nowhere. They were highly advanced technologically, capable of exceptional metallurgy, smelting, refining and alloying as well as petroleum fuel refining. How did this happen?

Sumeria was one of the first civilisations that recorded the creation of man in a sophisticated form by writing on clay tablets. In their belief system, God was an alien being and the human race was seeded by space travellers. These space travellers were described as gods and angels, fiery chariots and other inexplicable phenomena. They were known as the *Anunnaki* or 'those who from heaven to earth came'.

As a result of the intervention of the Anunnaki, humans developed and advanced as a race. In modern-day terms, the Anunnaki performed genetic engineering to create the human race.

That gives us one explanation why their civilisation was so far advanced – that is, alien races wanted to use our DNA in some way and this was initally the sole purpose of their visitation.

Early versions of hybrid races may not have been as succesful as initially hoped for. Imagine human hybrids – the result of supernatural beings (Anunnaki), who interbred with human women who roamed the Earth before the Great Flood in The Bible (Noah's flood). In The Bible these hybrids are known as the *Nephilim*. Some of the mutations or offspring resulted in giants such as Goliath and Cyclops in the Greek myths – giants who walked the Earth and helped humans create great monuments with their enormous strength. Think impossibly created Egyptian pyramids, the amazing Sphinx, the majestic Easter Island statues and other huge structures that defy logic as to how they were created given the basic tools and knowledge of the time.

Were humans given a helping hand in achieving great feats that advanced our civilisation?

Darwin's Theory of Evolution

If there was no alien interference, how were humans created?

It is commonly belived that humans evolved from ape ancestors 600,000 years ago. That means that ancient primates were the first humans. What makes this theory complex and debatable is just 'how' this process of evolution take place. That is, a long-term process that results in better-adapted individuals, who reproduce more successfully.

You may know this theory by another name – 'survival of the fittest'. What does this mean exactly? Favourable mutations allow organisms to survive in extreme conditions and to pass this new advantage on to the next generation. It is disputed that hominids (great apes) evolved into homo sapiens naturally – it is, rather, suggested that this change was a unique feature and that no other animal had made such a quantum leap.

But not all agree with Darwin. Other scientists argue that evolution is not based on random selection criteria and that all changes have a creative intelligence behind them.

How did modern human cognitive abilities come about so quickly? It was only 50,000 years ago that the genes of ancient humans went through a big change in brain development. This phenomenon was called 'the big brain event'. Was it genetic manipulation? Some theorists claim that it was alien interference and that they integrated alien DNA into the genome of the most advanced life form at the time, in this case the hominid. This resulted in reasonably fast brain development with each subsequent generation.

In all Sumerian texts it is clear that it took more than one experiment to create the right human. There were various versions of hominids until we had homo sapiens with a unique feature other than superior intelligence – the gift of language. Did extra-terrestrials insert this special gene in us? And, if so, was it to advance our level of communication with each other and with the alien species?

If humans received a jump-start from aliens, it would explain how we developed in a relatively short period of time and would resolve the 'missing link' theory.

The Garden of Eden: A lab for creating humans

Let's revisit Sumeria and The Bible. Could genetic experimentation have taken place in the Garden of Eden (in Sumerian, Eden means 'flat terrain'), also known as 'the garden of the gods'? Is this the place where Adam and Eve were the first working models that were used to procreate the rest of humanity? Was this place real?

Translations tell us that it was a walled garden with a perfect environment. In other words, it may have been a biosphere, as we know it today. Oddly enough, the Eden Project in Cornwall contains the world's largest geodesic domes that have two distinct biospheres – the humid tropical biome and the warm temperate biome, featuring plant species from all over the world.

In The Bible, four specific rivers surrounding the Garden of Eden are mentioned, and researchers believe that the location of the Garden of Eden is the Persian Gulf. Keep in mind that when the ice caps melted, the Indian Ocean flooded the land and flooded the Gulf. It seems to match ancient stories that the Garden of Eden was indeed destroyed in the Great Flood.

Some speculate that the tree of knowledge was really the DNA sequencing in our bodies, engineered by aliens, and if we had the knowledge of how to do this ourselves, we too would be 'like the gods'. Apparently there was disagreement among the alien gods about passing this knowledge on to humans.

Man-god is not always a perfect combination

Erich von Däniken writes about many examples of the mixing of gods and human races:

> 'The Incas held that they were the descendants of the "sons of the Sun".
>
> From India comes the Mahabharata and other ancient Sanskrit texts, which tell of gods begetting

children with women of Earth, and how these children inherited the supernatural skills and learning of their fathers.

An early Persian myth tells that before the coming of Zoroaster, demons had corrupted the Earth, and allied themselves with women.

In the Sumerian Epic of Gilgamesh the "watchers" from outer space came to planet Earth, and produced giants.'

The interbreeding between gods and humans came to an end with the Great Flood.

Sumerian tablet depicting Enki in the creation myth

Nibiru and Planet X

The Sumerians recorded that their 'gods' came from the planet Nibiru – 'Planet of the Crossing' possibly from our own solar system. This planet was also known as the 12th planet. Later, the Assyrians and Babylonians called it 'Marduk' (after a supreme Babylonian god). Nibiru was represented by a winged disc – a common image of the sun and of a sun god.

There has not been evidence to prove that Nibiru, the 12th planet is a possibility. Astronomers have only recently discovered a 9th planet, known as 'Planet X'. This new celestial body is nearly the size of Neptune, but is not yet visible as it lurks beyond Pluto and orbits the sun every 15,000 years.

Planet X is not Nibiru (the 12th planet) but the fact that it is a recent discovery could mean that there may be a 12th planet yet to be discovered. Could the ancient Sumerians have been right all along?

Our problem with understanding the ancients is that their stories were told as myths. They used images and pictographs to depict their gods – such as the Sun god – as beings and not celestial bodies to explain our solar system. We have yet to discover what is truth and what is fiction. The point is, how did a civilisation gain advanced knowledge of astronomy, describing planets in the solar system such as Uranus and Neptune that were only discovered by science in recent history?

Enoch and the Hybrids

Ever wondered why Noah's Ark and the Great Flood happened? We need to look at his great-grandfather, Enoch, to find out.

Enoch was the seventh patriarch from Adam: his son was Methuselah, his grandson was Lamech, and his great-grandson was none other than Noah.

Enoch is the first human ever to be taken to 'heaven'- Genesis 5:24. Could Enoch have been communicating with extra-terrestrials, and possibly taken away for good to another planet?

According to the Book of the Watchers (1 Enoch 1-36), some of their group of angels were sent to Earth to watch the humans, but 200 of them had sexual contact with humans and created the Nephilim. These Watchers are known as the 'fallen angels'.

The giants that resulted from this union were savages who destroyed lives and even resorted to cannibalism. There was no other way but for the 'gods' to destroy the Earth to finally get rid of the genetic mutation gone wrong. Simple solution – the Nephilim had to go.

And so we have the story of Noah and the Great Flood – the catastrophic flood that destroys the Earth, except for Noah and his ark with his family and all of Earth's creatures (or perhaps it was just their DNA). Researchers are looking at evidence of a disruption in the solar system around this time. Was the Earth's orbit disrupted by some collision causing great floods?

Whatever caused the Great Flood, it did not kill off the giants. Some theorise that Noah had 'good' alien DNA and passed it on to his descendants. Others say that his son's wife had Nephilim genes or the mutated DNA. The giants are mentioned later in The Bible in Joshua's Canaan battle. Could they still be roaming the Earth today?

How were the Hybrids identified?

The best evidence we have today of giants and other potential alien–human hybrid species are bone remains – giant skeletons and skulls in America claimed to have been found in the last few hundred years. In 1833, at Lompock Rancho in California, soldiers digging a powder magazine pit found the skeleton of a 3.6-metre giant. Not only was he huge, but he had remarkable double rows of front teeth and was buried with numerous stone axes, carved shells, and porphyry blocks (rocks containing large crystals) with mysterious symbols. The skeleton and artefacts were reburied and the location was lost over time.

There were many other giant skeleton discoveries in the early 1900s in Nevada and Pennsylvania. Today the giant skull of Lovelock Cave found in Nevada in 1911 still exists and is preserved.

Were these the same race as the Nephilim or the giants of The Bible?

While we are on the subject of skulls, we only have to look to ancient Egypt to see the beginnings of alien culture. The skulls depicted on hieroglyphs were even stranger than the giant skulls.

Pharaoh Akhenaten – the cone-head king

Pharaoh Amenhotep IV, more commonly known as the heretical Pharaoh Akhenaten, was Egypt's rebel pharaoh, and because of his position he had the power to make changes. This is exactly what he did. He changed the faith from Amun-Ra to the one 'true' god of Aten (the Sun disc), and in this one swift move created the first monotheistic religion (one god). He went further and changed his name to Akhenaten, which means 'the glory of Aten'.

But luck ran out for Pharaoh Akhenaten. Those who believed in the old religion were not prepared to convert to the 'one god' belief and, eventually, Akhenaten's son, Tutankhamen, restored the old system. Akhenaten married Nefertiti, an Egyptian woman whose parentage is unknown, her name not listed prior to her marriage. This is in itself mysterious, but stranger still is that both Nefertiti and Akhenaten are always portrayed with strange, elongated skulls, which gives rise to a theory that they have alien origins. This distinguishing feature supports the theory that the royal couple may have been of alien origin and therefore hybrids.

Other factors, such as their children also having elongated skulls, their willingness to practise to single-god worship, their disappearance from historical records and missing bodies all contribute to these theories. It's also very odd that all physical traces of them have disappeared, and nothing is known about their death. Akhenaten is the only Pharaoh of the 18th dynasty whose mummy has not been found, and after their deaths and disappearances – Nefertiti earlier than Akhenaten – they were never mentioned again in any historical records. Their tombs were discovered in the 1890s, but they were empty. It was as if the tombs were never used.

All of this evidence has led many to assume that Akhenaten and Nefertiti weren't ordinary people, maybe not even ordinary humans. Some believe that Akhenaten may have been the last Pharaoh entrusted with sacred (and alien) knowledge of stargates and anti-gravity technologies.

If that's the case, where did that knowledge go? Is it hidden somewhere beneath the sands of Egypt with his body and that of his wife? Were their bodies and the information taken away by the very beings who gave it to them? I guess we'll have to wait for the next great archaeological discovery to find out.

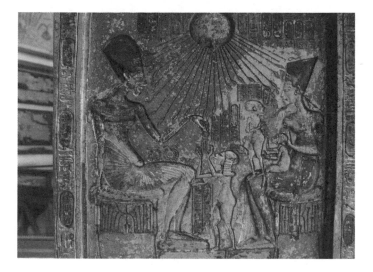

The Lost Continents

Is it mere legend or have entire continents and civilisations
sunk beneath the waves ages ago – from biblical tales of Noah's
Great Flood to Plato's discourse on Atlantis and Churchward's
theory of Lemuria? Science does not support these stories, not
because they are not possible but because they don't fit into the
accepted timeline of when civilisations first began.

Many coastal cities were destroyed by rising waters at the
end of the ice age. Survivors of the floods would have moved
to higher ground or migrated somewhere else altogether. But
is it just coastal cities that sank or perhaps whole continents?

Atlantis

Before the Sumerians there were two legendary worlds of advanced civilisations – Lemuria (Mu) and Atlantis. Both of these continents were examples of an idyllic society: they had advanced technological knowledge for the time and enjoyed riches beyond that of any other civilisation that followed. But both continents had a tragic fate: both were destroyed and sank to the depths of the ocean due to a cataclysmic natural disaster.

But what of their remains? These lands were considered mythical realms where alien intervention helped to create a fairytale paradise. But as our technology becomes more sophisticated, it has allowed us to venture to the depths of the ocean and discover the mysteries of the lost lands.

The legend of the lost island of Atlantis has captured our imaginations since the time of Plato, the ancient Greek philosopher, who wrote an account of an island that had an advanced technological civilisation and existed around 9600 BCE. Plato wrote about Atlantis over 2300 years ago in his literary works, the *Timaeus* and *Critias*.

The entire island was said to have disappeared into the Atlantic Ocean in 'a single day and night' of earthquakes and floods. But could it be explained as a series of natural disasters with floods and tidal waves caused by earthquakes from a volcano on the island? Or perhaps an asteroid strike? If so, no trace of this level of catastrophe has been found.

It is said that alien ships colonised the continent of Atlantis and interbred with humans. The question is, why was it destroyed?

There are more questions than answers when it comes to Atlantis. Did aliens become alarmed that alien–human hybrids were out of control – given that they began to wage war against neighbouring countries with their advanced weaponry and huge naval forces? Was the allegiance to their mother planet weakened and a decision was made to evacuate the colony and destroy all traces of alien presence on Earth? Were nuclear weapons responsible for its destruction, given that no traces of Atlantis have been found? Was the lost continent of Atlantis vaporised in a nuclear attack by aliens who wanted to destroy all evidence of their landing on Earth?

Summary of Plato's writings

This is a summary of the story told by Plato around 360 BCE in his dialogues *Timaeus* and *Critias*. These writings of Plato are the only known references to Atlantis:

> 'Over 11,000 years ago there existed an island nation located in the middle of the Atlantic Ocean populated by a noble and powerful race.

Atlantis was the domain of Poseidon, god of the sea.

When Poseidon fell in love with a mortal woman, Cleito, he created a dwelling at the top of a hill near the middle of the island and surrounded the dwelling with rings of water and land to protect her.

Cleito gave birth to five sets of twin boys who became the first rulers of Atlantis.

The island was divided among the brothers with the eldest, Atlas, first King of Atlantis, being given control over the central hill and surrounding areas.

To facilitate travel and trade, a water canal was cut through the rings of land and water and ran south for 5.5 miles (9 kilometres) to the sea.

For generations the Atlanteans lived simple, virtuous lives. But slowly they began to change. Greed and power began to corrupt them. When Zeus saw the immorality of the Atlanteans he gathered the other gods to determine a suitable punishment.

Soon, in one violent surge, it was gone. The island of Atlantis, its people, and its memory were swallowed by the sea.'

Suppose we substitute ancient gods, such as Poseidon, with an alien being. His wife is human and their children are hybrids. We would have a totally different perspective. Why did Poseidon have to 'protect' his human wife and children? Why did he build concentric circles of water for their protection? How did they learn the advanced method of irrigation, building and engineering? Was Zeus indeed an alien leader (the supreme god) and decided that loyalty to the mother planet was now divided? His only option was to destroy the colony and prevent future interbreeding? Familiar? It sounds a lot like the Great Flood of The Bible – the Earth destroyed due to people's greed and corruption.

Where was Atlantis?

Consider the possibility that there may have been a land mass connecting the continents together, rather than Atlantis being an island in the Atlantic. In the *Timaeus,* Plato said Atlantis was 'the way to other islands, and from these you might pass to the whole of the opposite continent'.

This may explain the 'coincidence' by which ancient cultures seemed to have acquired certain knowledge and skills that were beyond their level of development at the time, particularly in the areas of engineering. This seems evident considering the sophisticated irrigation systems and the canals described by Plato. According to Erich von Däniken, it is possible that the Atlanteans were the original pyramid builders, and they shared their knowledge with their neighbours. This would explain the presence of pyramid structures across continents, from ancient Egypt in Africa all the way to the Mayans in South America. Was Atlantis, therefore, a huge continent somewhere in the Atlantic Ocean that formed a bridge between other continents?

Bimini Road and Spartel Island

When renowned psychic Edgar Cayce (1877–1945) performed past-life regressions, many of his clients reported that they'd led previous lives in Atlantis, giving him detailed descriptions of the civilisation. Cayce also made his own prediction of when and where the remains of Atlantis would be found:

> 'A portion of the temples [of Atlantis] may yet be discovered under the slime of ages and sea water near Bimini … Expect it in '68 or '69; not so far away.'

Sure enough, in 1968 (some 23 years after Cayce's own death) the Bimini Road was discovered in less than 15 feet (4.5 metres) of water on the floor of the Atlantic Ocean, at North Bimini Island in the Bahamas.

The Bimini Road is a half-mile-long (almost a kilometre) road of perfectly aligned limestone rocks that end in a 90-degree bend. Viewed from the air, it looks more like a low wall than a road. Additional evidence, based on how these stones were cut with laser precision, points to them being man-made by a highly civilised culture. Not a natural phenomenon as first thought.

Another Atlantean location is Spartel Island. It only lies a shallow 60 metres underwater, west of the Straights of Gibraltar (also known as the Pillars of Heracles/Hercules).

Plato described this exact place also as Atlantis:

'There was an island situated in front of the Pillars of Hercules; the island was larger than Libya and Asia put together, [it was] the way to other islands, and from these you might pass to the whole of the opposite continent.'

There is geological evidence to suggest that Spartel Island was destroyed by earthquakes and floods around 11,600 years ago.

Where does this leave us? How can the lost land of Atlantis be found in more than one place and at opposite sides of the ocean? Perhaps the answer might just lie in the theory that Atlantis was not a single country but a large continent, much larger than continents today. It may even have been the ancient supercontinent, Pangaea. Given that the ten sons of Poseidon ruled Atlantis, it could not have simply been as small an island as Plato described. You could assume that only a huge country would need ten people to rule it.

The theory that aliens may have destroyed it with nuclear weapons in order to reduce it in size seems to be no less viable than any other explanation. The question remains why.

Lemuria

For thousands of years the Polynesians have told the story of a continent in the Pacific that was the motherland of mankind. It was much earlier than Atlantis, estimated to have existed as early as 200,000 years ago, and most of its life was aquatic in the beginning. This fits with what we know of the Theory of Evolution.

According to explorer James Churchward, Lemuria was once located in the Pacific Ocean and stretched from the Hawaiian Islands to Fiji and from Easter Island to the Mariana Islands – about 5,000 miles (8,000 kilometres) long and 3,000 miles (5,000 kilometres) wide. It's what is known as The Pacific Ring of Fire, where, even today, tectonic plates on the Earth's surface cause earthquakes, tsunamis and volcanoes.

Author David Childress states that the very first civilisation arose 78,000 years ago on a giant continent known as Mu or Lemuria, and lasted for an astonishing 52,000 years. It was then destroyed by earthquakes after a pole shift, which occurred approximately 24,000 BCE.

Did the people of Lemuria perish?

Unlike the Atlanteans, the Lemurian 'prophets' had information that there was going to be an unavoidable natural disaster. And that disaster was in the form of the Great Flood. They prepared for this cataclysm thousands of years before and began to preserve their knowledge in specially made underground structures, storing the information in various forms such as maps and crystals to help establish new advanced civilisations after the flood.

When the flood came, the selected ones took refuge underground and emerged from the earth only when it was safe to do so. Those saved reached India and, from there, travelled to Mesopotamia and Egypt – while others migrated eastward on basic rafts to the Americas, forming the beginnings of the earliest ancient Native American tribes.

Native American legend describes this mass exodus:

'On the bottom of the seas lie all the proud cities, the flying patuwvotas (shields) and the worldly treasures corrupted with evil. Faced with disaster, some people hid inside the earth while others escaped by crossing the ocean on reed rafts, using the islands as stepping-stones.'

Churchward believed that major civilisations sprang from Lemuria. It was the common origin of ancient Egypt, Greece, Central America, India, Burma and other areas like Easter Island.

Theories about Lemurian culture

Lemuria was said to have 13 colonies and it was the Lemurians who decided that Atlantis would be a chosen colony for the creation and birth of a new civilisation. It was where ancient Lemurian knowledge would be taught.

The Elders of Lemuria, known as the 13th School, moved their headquarters before the disaster to the then uninhabited plateau of Central Asia (now Tibet). Here they established a library and school known as The Great White Brotherhood.

Stone monuments of mysterious origin dot the entire Pacific. There are underwater sites in Yonaguni, Japan, strange petroglyphs on Hawaii's Big Island, and the famous monolithic stone statues of Easter Island.

Many believe that Easter Island was part of Lemuria. Its hundreds of giant stone statues and written language suggest an advanced culture, yet it appeared on the world's most remote spot. Legend tells of a place called Hiva, near Easter Island, which sank beneath the waves as people fled. Science has yet to confirm the probable existence of Lemuria, but as our technology becomes ever more sophisticated, we will find more answers. We only have to look at biblical literature to see that there is more to stories than is immediately obvious.

Ancient Aircraft and Astronauts

Ezekiel's Wheel, 593 BCE – A UFO encounter

One of the most quoted UFO incidents from The Bible is Ezekiel's Wheel.

'This was the appearance and structure of the wheels: They sparkled like chrysolite, and all four looked alike. Each appeared to be made like a wheel intersecting a wheel.'

Ezekiel 1:16

Former NASA engineer Josef Blumrich, author of *The Spaceships of Ezekiel,* analysed Ezekiel's account and compared it to modern-day spacecraft, saying that it could have been a small part of an alien spaceship.

'I looked, and I saw a windstorm coming out of the north – an immense cloud with flashing lightning and surrounded by brilliant light. The centre of the fire looked like glowing metal.'

Ezekiel 1:4

Blumrich interprets this to be the spacecraft beginning its descent from quite a distance – the vapour cloud is a result of the act of cooling the jets before firing the rocket engine. He goes on to explain that the rocket engine when fired creates the brilliant light and glowing metal. It's uncanny that the main body of the craft is similar to UFOs witnessed today – the surface of the main body is metallic and bright. Very much like Ezekiel witnessed.

'Spread out above the heads of the living creatures (craft engines) was what looked like an expanse, sparkling like ice.'

Ezekiel 1:22

Did Ezekiel witness an extra-terrestrial encounter? Were these beings sent by 'God' to deliver a message? Perhaps Ezekiel may have gone aboard the craft and interacted with the commander? Truth or fiction? Sometimes in what we consider to be narrative and myth, the ancients were in fact recording what they saw in the context of their day, and their simple concepts are not in the language of Earth's twenty-first century.

Indian Flying Machines

References to flying machines, known as *vimanas*, are common in ancient Indian texts, even describing their use in warfare. As well as being able to fly within Earth's atmosphere, vimanas were also said to be able to travel into space and travel under water. The encyclopaedic work on classical Indian architecture and sculptural objects, the *Samarangana Sutradhara of Bhojadeva*, describes the flying machines as bird-shaped aerial cars. They were made of light material, with a strong, well-shaped body. Iron, copper, mercury and lead were used in their construction. They could fly to great distances and were propelled through air by motors.

It's not your usual flying craft an Indian population would be exposed to thousands of years ago. Artistic licence or factual information?

Ancient Landing Strips

The city of Teotihuacan, 'the place where the gods were created', sits some 50 kilometres (31 miles) north-east of Mexico City. It was built between the first and seventh centuries CE and is renowned for its huge monuments, in particular the Temple of Quetzalcoatl and the Pyramids of the Sun and the Moon, which are laid out on geometric and symbolic principles.

Alien landing strips

The Pyramids, there, are different from other Mesoamerican pyramids. They don't have any chambers on top. Instead they have a flat top designed as some kind of landing platform – only vertical. This would suggest that, unlike a plane that needs a runway, the aircraft that may have landed here was able to hover and land directly onto the platforms. An alien spacecraft would have this capability. According to UFOlogists, these may well have been landing hubs for alien spacecraft.

Golden Aircraft

These flying birds crafted from gold look more like aircraft than stylised birds. Did the Aztecs, Mayans and Incas witness aircraft in operation?

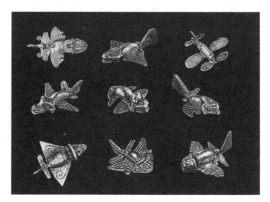

A gold bird or gold aircraft?

The ancient Mesoamericans also made statues that resemble pilots in space suits, as evidenced by these pictures.

Ancient pilots

Perhaps the most astonishing artefact of ancient astronauts is the one depicted on the carved stone that covers the tomb of Pakal Votan, who once ruled Palenque city, Mexico, around 603–683 CE. You will see that he is sitting in the cockpit of some compact aerial vehicle and he is operating levers or joysticks. It is generally agreed that it resembles a modern engine and its exhaust system.

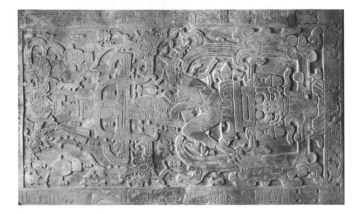

Art Depicting UFOs

Never mind the drama of the crucifixion in this artwork – look at what's going on in the skies. Not only do we see a UFO, but the artist shows us who's inside it! 'The Crucifixion', painted in 1350, depicts a small human looking over his shoulder at another UFO in pursuit as he flies across the sky in what is clearly a spaceship. The painting hangs above the altar at the Visoki Decani Monastery in Kosovo. Why hasn't this controversial painting ever been given more attention and critique in art history?

The Palazzo Vecchio in Florence houses the painting of the 'Madonna and Saint Giovannino'. Zooming in, you can clearly see a bright disc-like object in the daytime sky. The artist draws our eye to the UFO object more directly by the man watching it with his dog. Have art lovers over history ever wondered what a flying machine was doing in a painting created in the 1500s?

'The Baptism of Christ' was painted in 1710, by Aert De Gelder. This is one of the finest UFO and alien depictions in ancient art: a flying saucer hovering over the scene with beams of light shining down on Christ as John baptises him. It could be interpreted as a divine being, but its uncanny resemblance to common UFO descriptions leaves little doubt about what it was.

Despite scientific scepticism, records of art history contain examples of mysterious objects being sighted in the sky. What are these ancient artefacts trying to tell us about the origins of humanity? Do they suggest a missing piece in the history of the human story? The extraterrestrial depictions in art remain controversial – but is it too far-fetched to believe that they could be taken literally?

Part Two

UFOs – How Aliens Have Landed On Earth

'I imagine they might exist in massive ships, having used up all the resources from their home planet. Such advanced aliens would perhaps become nomads, looking to conquer and colonise whatever planets they can reach … If aliens ever visit us, I think the outcome would be much as when Christopher Columbus first landed in America, which didn't turn out very well for the American Indians.'

Stephen Hawking

The universe contains hundreds of billions of galaxies, each with hundreds of millions of stars, many of which have been shown to have planets in orbit. Discoveries made through the Kepler Space Telescope indicate that about one in five bodies orbiting the stars similar to our sun could be the size and mass of the Earth. That means there could be more than ten billion habitable planets in the Milky Way alone. No longer just one universe, we now exist in a multiverse (more than one universe). Our entire universe is insignificant on the cosmic scale. It is just one of the countless universes, each doing its very own thing

For those who argue against the idea of a multiverse, they should consider this question: if we were alone in the universe, wouldn't it be such a huge waste of space? And even if there were the possibility of extra-terrestrial life on other planets, might they be very different to our own?

According to astrophysicist Stephen Hawking,

> 'To my mathematical brain, the numbers alone make thinking about aliens perfectly rational. The real challenge is to work out what aliens might actually be like.'

Hawking suggests that, based on examples of life surviving on Earth in extreme environments, life could be found in unbelievable places such as in the centre of stars or even floating in interplanetary space. Evidence suggests that Mars was once a wetter, warmer planet, with its northern hemisphere covered in a great ocean. Could there be some simple life beneath its surface?

But what if an intelligent life-form existed in the cosmos? What would that mean for us? Hawking clearly thinks it would spell disaster for the human race.

Our universe, then, is possibly overflowing with other life and civilisations, but we just haven't yet documented their existence. Sightings of unusual movements in the sky, both at night and during daylight hours, have occurred as long as humans have lived on earth. And continue to do so on a daily basis.

Portals and Wormholes: How science explains UFOs

NASA-sponsored research is being developed to find a way for spacecraft to detect hidden magnetic portals near Earth. These portals link the magnetic field of our planet to that of the sun. If portals could be proved to exist, it may explain the erratic and short duration of UFO sightings. It's been suggested that UFOs reveal themselves just prior to entering or exiting a portal. It makes one wonder if portals exist between galaxies as well as between Earth and the sun. If they did, it could provide a plausible explanation as to why we have not found intelligent life in the Milky Way and proof that there may be life in other parts of the universe or other galaxies that use these portals for intergalactic space travel.

And then there are wormholes. A wormhole is, in theory, a passage through space-time that creates shortcuts for long journeys across the universe or multiverse. Physicists and mathematicians have used the theory of general relativity to suggest the possibility of the existence of 'bridges' through space-time. If this were indeed possible, it would explain the unpredictable sightings of UFOs at various times in our earth's history.

So What Does a UFO Look Like?

A UFO, by definition, is an 'unidentified flying object'. It does not necessarily mean alien life-forms; only that the object is not one that the viewer can identify.

Sometimes sightings of what were labelled flying saucers and alien spacecraft lights have been later identified as weather balloons, light reflecting fog or clouds, distress flares, ventricular clouds, plane vapour trails, plasma, ball lightning, meteors and low-flying aeroplanes.

Regardless of the shape of the spacecraft, here are some common features in sightings of UFOs:

- Unusual colour and pattern
- Intense and pulsating lights
- Completing a big circuit

- Moving quickly and performing radical manoeuvres that are impossible in known aircraft
- Moving erratically
- Three aircraft flying in a triangle formation

Case Study 1: First flying saucer

By far the UFO that's captured everyone's imagination is the flying saucer. During the crazy UFO sightings of 1947, amateur pilot Kenneth Arnold was flying a small plane when he sighted nine flying disc-shaped objects near Mt Rainier, in Washington state, USA.

They flew between two mountains spaced 50 miles (80 kilometres) apart in just 1 minute, 42 seconds, he observed, implying an astonishing speed of 1,700 miles (2,735 kilometres) per hour, or three times faster than any manned aircraft of the era. However, as if controlled, the flying objects seemed to dip and swerve around obstacles in the terrain.

Arnold had told the press that the objects had flown erratically, 'like a saucer if you skip it across the water'. They were thin and flat when viewed on edge, he said, but crescent-shaped when viewed from the top down as they turned.

Soon everyone was looking for these new aircraft, which, according to the papers, were saucer-like in shape. Within weeks hundreds of reports of these flying saucers were made across the nation.

Case Study 2: An astronomer sights a UFO and strange green fireballs

Clyde Tombaugh was the American astronomer who discovered the planet Pluto. As a highly skilled professional, it could be said that his chances of wrongly identifying a UFO were highly unlikely.

Tombaugh reported having seen three mysterious green fireballs, which suddenly appeared over New Mexico in late 1948. These strange objects continued to be sighted through the early 1950s. In 1956, Tombaugh had the following to say:

> 'I have seen three objects in the last seven years which defied any explanation of known phenomenon, such as Venus, atmospheric optic, meteors or planes. I am a highly skilled, professional astronomer. In addition I have seen three green fireballs which were unusual in behavior from normal green fireballs ... I think that several reputable scientists are being unscientific in refusing to entertain the possibility of extra-terrestrial origin and nature.'

On 20 August 1949, he observed a UFO that appeared as a geometrically arranged group of six to eight rectangles of light. They were window-like in appearance and yellowish-green in colour; and moved from north-west to south-east over Las Cruces, New Mexico:

'I doubt that the phenomenon was any terrestrial reflection, because ... nothing of the kind has ever appeared before or since ... I was so unprepared for such a strange sight that I was really petrified with astonishment.'

UFO individual case studies

Anna's story

This sighting occurred in South Gippsland, Victoria, on a dairy farm:

'It was a clear evening on our dairy farm. At first everything looked in order, but then I noticed something quite remarkable. A flying saucer was hovering over the milking shed. The shape of this was just like an upside-down plate, just like many are depicted. It had alternating green and red lights on the edge of the UFO. The UFO appeared white but was quite luminous.

It was very silent with just a faint flutter sound. The UFO wasn't very large but spanned over the milking shed roof and was circular in shape. It may have been about 20 metres or so high.

Our house was perched on a little hill and below us were some flat plains. The UFO moved and flew over the flats and back over the house a few times. The UFO was very low to the ground. It stayed around for about 20 minutes and then it vanished!

It was not a scary experience at all. It felt like we were being checked on. This has been a profound experience all my life. I recall this sighting almost daily.'

Mike's tale

Mike heard a humming noise. A luminous bright light filtered through the curtained windows. Tasmania is well-known for its UFO sightings and Mike wanted to experience one for himself – maybe this was it! It was only weeks ago that his friend had been chased by UFOs as he was driving down the lonely highway.

What happened next was not what he'd expected – and the image has haunted him all his life:

'I pulled back the curtain to see a cigar-shaped ship with the tall aliens sitting in seats and looking out of the ship. I quickly closed the curtains again and waited for twenty minutes before I could move. By then the spacecraft had gone.'

A Tasmanian experience

The Great Western Tiers in Northern Tasmania is an amazingly rich and ancient landscape, with towering cliffs, lakes and tall forests. The traditional Aboriginal owners of this land know it as The Home of the Spirits or Land of the Spirits.

The Great Western Tiers is known for the unusual lights that have been seen over this mountain range. Locals have witnessed orbs of silver, red or white light.

One probable reason for UFOs being attracted to this part of the world may be related to their attraction to the Earth's magnetic field. Another is the remoteness of the area. Not far from this region, UFOs have been seen hovering between mobile-phone towers, using the energy power. An extra boost (or just eavesdropping)?

If statistics are right – that a UFO is sighted somewhere every three minutes – could there be many more unreported sightings? What if for each newsworthy UFO sighting there were countless others not making the headlines?

UFOs That Made the Headlines

Nullarbor incident: Attacked by a UFO on the Nullarbor Plain, Australia

It was the road trip from hell. The Knowles family (a mother and her three adult sons) were driving the epic 2, 730-kilometre (1,696 miles) journey from Perth to Melbourne.

Sean Knowles, the driver, noticed an object that looked like an egg in an egg cup – it was glowing white with yellow tinges around the edges. It disappeared and then reappeared, flying low and suddenly about to collide with their car.

He swerved to avoid the object and came to a screeching halt. The object had disappeared. So he thought. Above them a glow engulfed their car. It made a strange whirring hum, like an engine, but it was so loud that it shook their car.

A fine layer of black dust rushed in through the window. The car seemed to be rising up into the air, drawn by some kind of magnetic force. Then it fell with a crash, crunching the undercarriage.

A tyre burst and the car swerved out of control and crashed into some saltbushes on the side of the road.

The Knowles family jumped out, terrified and distressed, and hid in the bushes until the object flew away.

Other drivers reported that they too had seen strange lights that night on the same stretch of road.

This strange encounter remains a mystery even today.

School Hysteria: Westall High School, Melbourne, 6 April 1966

Students and teachers of Westall High School reported two disc-shaped objects descending from the sky and landing in an open field next to the school. One object was described as being silver-green.

A few students ran across the oval to the empty field to get a closer look. According to some, it took another twenty minutes before the UFOs took off, leaving a burnt patch of ground where the aircraft had apparently landed. There were over 200 people who claim to have witnessed this and fifty years later there is still a sense of mystery surrounding this sighting.

Was this just a case of some hyper-excited kids and teachers blowing the story out of proportion?

What made it front-page news was that it was the first mass sighting in Australia. On top of that, students reported being confronted by men in sharp black suits, who warned them against talking. Emergency services and military swarmed the area.

One explanation was that the objects were part of a secret testing project known as the HIBAL program. It consisted of large silver-white balloons equipped with sensors and a parachute, used to monitor atmospheric radiation levels.

It's a logical explanation, except that the paperwork for the launches scheduled for that day has either been lost or destroyed. And the children who witnessed the strange phenomenon, and who are now middle-aged adults, still claim to have seen flying saucers on that day.

The incident has left such an impression on the community that the 'landing site' has since been turned into a memorial park to reflect the events of 6 April 1966.

What's That in the Sky?

Millions of people have seen strange objects in the sky that appear, dissolve, reappear, change shape, and change direction for no apparent reason. These UFOs cannot all be explained as planes, weather balloons, drones, or satellites. Not all the time. Large-scale sightings have occurred on all continents and capital cites including Mexico City, Buenos Aires, Tokyo, London and others. But as strange as it sounds, these detections have been sensationalised to the point of them being criticised as a hoax, despite photos proving their existence. It doesn't help matters that it's been standard practice in almost every country for government agencies to dismiss such sightings as ordinary events.

Anything is possible, and just because we haven't found other intelligent life-forms it doesn't mean they do not exist. Astronaut Edgar D. Mitchell gives us an insight into his view of the history of UFOs and alien visitations:

'Yes, there have been ET visitations. There have been crashed craft. There have been material and bodies recovered. There has been a certain amount of reverse engineering that has allowed some of these craft, or some components, to be duplicated. And there is some group of people that may or may not be associated with government at this point that have this knowledge. They have been attempting to conceal this knowledge. People in high level government have very little, if any, valid information about this. It has been the subject of disinformation in order to deflect attention and create confusion so the truth doesn't come out.'

Edgar D. Mitchell, *The Way of the Explorer: An Apollo Astronaut's Journey Through the Material and Mystical Worlds*

Conspiracy Theory

A UFO conspiracy theory is any one which argues that evidence of the reality of UFOs is being suppressed by various governments around the world. The common belief is that governments, especially the United States, are in communication and cooperation with extra-terrestrials, including the sanctioning of alien abductions.

See more at: http://www.educatinghumanity.com

The Disclosure Project

So how far have we come with investigating the UFO and alien theories?

Where would you find an organisation with over 500 government, military and intelligence community witnesses giving their testimony of first-hand experience with UFOs, ETs, ET technology, and the cover-ups that keep this information secret?

It's known as the The Disclosure Project – a non-profit research project working to fully disclose these hidden facts. There are many people listed in this project who are speaking out.

Since the introduction of The Disclosure Project, the public are now entitled to an intelligent response from authorities. The term 'Disclosure' has come to be associated with the hiding of information about the presence on Earth of intelligent life from other planets. Spokespeople for Disclosure believe that our government agencies, particularly the military, have been keeping secrets concerning their interactions with extra-terrestrials since the 1940s.

Clifford Stone, a former army sergeant who worked at NATO, has revealed that the US Government had tried to suppress what he'd seen in Pennsylvania back in 1969.

'I was involved in situations where we actually did recoveries of crashed saucers. There were bodies that were involved with some of these crashes. Also some of these were alive … While we were doing this, we were telling the American public there was nothing to it. We were telling the world there was nothing to it.'

The Honourable Paul Hellyer was the Canadian Minister of National Defence in the 1960s during the cold war. He is the highest-ranking person among all G8 countries to openly speak about UFOs and extra-terrestrials.

Recently he disclosed that there are at least four known alien species that have been visiting Earth for thousands of years. His testimony is backed up by hundreds of other high-ranking military and political personnel all over the world, supported by official documents released by dozens of governments worldwide that have officially acknowledged the presence of UFOs.

Of the evidence, Hellyer says:

'In one of the cases during the cold war, 1961, there were about 50 UFOs in formation flying south from Russia across Europe. The supreme allied commander was very concerned and was about ready to press the panic button when they turned around and went back over the North Pole.

They decided to do an investigation and they investigated for three years and they decided that, with absolute certainty, that four different species, at least, have been visiting this planet for thousands of years. There's been a lot more activity in the past two decades, especially since we invented the atomic bomb. They are very concerned about that and if we will use it again, because the whole cosmos is a unity and it affects not just us but other people in the cosmos. They're very much afraid that we might start using atomic weapons again and this would be very bad for us, and them also.'

He describes aliens as:

'Many are benign and benevolent, and a few are not. They come from various places, for a long while I only knew about ones that came from different star systems, the Pleiades. There are extra-terrestrials that come from Andromeda, and ones that live on one of Saturn's moons. There is a federation of these people, and they have rules. One of them is that they don't interfere with our affairs unless they are invited. They have accepted the fact that this is our planet, and we have the right to run it, but they are very concerned, they don't think that we are good stewards of our planet. We are ruining our planet, we're doing all sorts of things that we shouldn't be doing, and they don't like that. They've made it clear, and they have given us a warning.'

And despite high-ranking officials declaring their involvement in alien cover-ups, there continues to be a trend that it is a conspiracy theory only and based on fiction. UFOlogists are not taken seriously in their reporting of UFOs and ETs.

Project Blue Book

Project Blue Book was the Air Force name for a project that investigated UFO reports between 1947 and 1969. During this time, a total of 12,618 sightings were reported to Project Blue Book. Of these, 701 remain 'unidentified'. The project was headquartered at Wright-Patterson Air Force Base, whose personnel no longer receive, document or investigate UFO reports.

Sergeant Stone says that Project Blue Book had another elite investigation unit thought to be working in conjunction with Blue Book but which actually was not. Stone has publicly stated that he has seen living and dead extra-terrestrials in his official duties on an army team that retrieved crashed ET craft.

However, Project Blue Book ended in 1969. The decision to discontinue UFO investigations was based on an evaluation of an official report from the national archives that concluded:

… no UFO reported, investigated and evaluated by the Air Force had ever given any indication of threat to national security

… there had been no evidence submitted to or discovered by the Air Force that sightings categorised as 'unidentified' represented technological developments or principles beyond the range of present-day scientific knowledge;

… and there had been no evidence indicating that sightings categorised as 'unidentified' were extra-terrestrial vehicles.

The national archives summary is that Project Blue Book
had no information on Roswell:

> 'The National Archives has been unable to locate any
> documentation among the Project Blue Book records
> which discuss the 1947 incident in Roswell, New Mexico.'

If that were indeed the case, then how can Roswell be
explained?

Investigating Roswell

Reports that an extra-terrestrial spacecraft and its alien
occupants were recovered near Roswell in July of 1947
were splashed across newspapers. The official response that
it was a weather balloon and that there were no aliens did
not dampen the public's curiosity. What was the truth?
According to an official inquiry, these were the findings on
8 September 1994.

- The Air Force research did not locate or develop any
  information that the 'Roswell Incident' was a UFO
  event, nor was there any indication of a 'cover-up, by the
  government.
- Information obtained through records and interviews
  indicate that the materials recovered near Roswell

were consistent with a surveillance or weather balloon of the type used in a then classified project, Project Mogul.

- No records indicated or even hinted at the recovery of 'alien' bodies or extra-terrestrial materials.

So what really happened at Roswell?

The basic chronology of the Roswell story is as follows:

Prequel – There had been unprecedented sighting of UFOs prior to the Roswell incident, with 16 recorded sightings occurring between 17 May and 12 July 1947. Some speculate there may have been up to 800 in total!

June 1947 – Rancher William (Mac) Brazel discovered
some unusual debris on his homestead just north of
Roswell, New Mexico. When interviewed by the *Roswell
Daily Record,* Brazel said he'd seen 'a large area of bright
wreckage made up of rubber strips, tinfoil, a rather tough
paper and sticks'. Brazel later said he'd previously found
two weather balloons on the ranch but this time the debris
did not resemble either of these. He thought no more of
it until he went back to the area with his wife, son and
daughter to gather the debris on 4 July.

4 July 1947 – Brazel reported to the local sheriff, George
Wilcox, that he might have recovered the remains of 'one of
them flying saucers'. Wilcox contacted military authorities
at nearby Roswell Army Air Field, where Major Jesse
Marcel was assigned to investigate.

Marcel and two Counter Intelligence Corps agents,
Sheridan Cavitt and Lewis Rickett, drove out to the ranch,
where Brazel worked to examine and collect the wreckage.

8 July 1947 – The public information office at Roswell AAF
announced that they had recovered the remains of a 'flying
disc'. According to the *Roswell Daily Record*, a Roswell
couple claimed to have seen a UFO fly by their home on
2 July 1947.

9 July 1947 – Brigadier General Roger Ramey, who
had ordered the wreckage sent to him for examination

at Carswell Air Force Base (Fort Worth), held a press conference, with Major Marcel present, and announced that it was a weather balloon. The story died. For a while, that is.

1978 – UFO researcher Stanton Friedman met Marcel, the Air Force Intelligence Officer in the Roswell affair, in order to dredge up the flying saucer story and expose the government's alleged cover-up.

8 December 1979 – Journalist Robert Pratt of the *National Inquirer* interviews Marcel, who claims that the wreckage material he'd recovered was 'nothing that came from Earth'. He described it as tissue-thin, indestructible metal with the 'I'-beams bearing some kind of hieroglyphics. The Roswell story was revived!

Variation of the Roswell Story: The dead aliens

The Roswell story morphed from one crash site to two crash sites where debris was collected. It was this second site where alien bodies were supposedly retrieved.

The alien bodies recovered from the Roswell crash site were rumoured to have been dead at the crash scene and taken back for autopsies to Area 51, a secret military location in Nevada.

The following stories, however, do not match and give rise to conspiracy theories.

In December 2002, Walter Haut, public information officer at Roswell base during the Roswell incident of July 1947, left an affidavit of what he claims happened:

> 'No one was able to identify the crash debris ... I was able to see a couple of bodies under a canvas tarpaulin. Only the heads extended beyond the covering ... the heads did appear larger than normal and the contour of the canvas suggested the size of a 10-year-old child.'

Truth or fantasy?

To make matters more complex, in 1995 film producer Ray Santilli revealed that he had genuine footage of the Roswell alien autopsy. However, this was later proved to be a hoax, with events that had been recreated. This was despite Santilli claiming that there were a few seconds of real footage.

The Air Force cover-up begins

Was the whole weather balloon scenario a cover-up by the military? Major Marcel, who was responsible for collecting the weather-balloon debris, makes an astonishing statement. He claims that the real debris from a flying saucer had been switched with ordinary weather-balloon remnants.

But was there a cover-up as Marcel claims, and was the weather balloon story part of that cover-up? According to Colonel Thomas J. DuBose, who was General Ramey's assistant, the weather-balloon story was indeed part of the cover-up. DuBose never knew what the Roswell object was, but he did know that it was not an ordinary weather balloon, contrary to what was claimed at that time.

If the Roswell incident did not involve the retrieval of wreckage from a genuine flying saucer, then why was the weather-balloon story given as an explanation? And what was the reason for the cover-up?

Answer – Project Mogul.

Project Mogul: The real answer

Project Mogul was a top-secret operation in 1947 that involved the use of weather balloons that were equipped with various instruments for intelligence-gathering purposes to spy on the then Soviet Union. It was the end of World War II and the US needed to know if the Russians were attempting to build nuclear weapons.

Because it was so top secret – not even those in the military knew of Project Mogul – this news couldn't get out for obvious reasons.

The Project Mogul team invented a number of high-tech materials for its balloons and other equipment, including ultra-lightweight and ultra-strong metals, fibre-optic cables and fireproof fabrics. Is it any wonder why people found it difficult to believe that these materials, never seen before, were not materials from outer space?

So, was Roswell hysteria caused by people who didn't know the identity of the recovered material, particularly as the discovery was during a time when the flying-saucer craze was sweeping America in 1947? Or is there more to the story than what was uncovered?

In 1994, the Pentagon de-classified most of its files on Project Mogul, and the federal General Accounting Office produced a report named the 'Report of Air Force Research Regarding the Roswell Incident', which was designed to debunk these rumours. However, hundreds of thousands of curious visitors go to Roswell and the crash site every year, hoping to find the truth for themselves.

Majestic 12 (MJ-12)

It sounds like a blockbuster movie title, but *Majestic 12* was the code name for a covert committee consisting of 12 members made up of military leaders, scientists and government officials, formed in 1947 under US President Harry S. Truman. It was formed for one reason only – to investigate the Roswell crash. In 1980, official documents came into existence which excited UFOlogists. The documents contained all sorts of information and instructions on what to do when meeting an alien, diagrams of UFOs and how to maintain security status. But the most extraordinary thing was that the papers had two very significant signatures – those of Albert Einstein and former president Ronald Reagan. These papers were considered to be fakes that had somehow slipped into the archives. Many claim that they are authentic.

In 1978, Canadian authorities also released their documents dating from 1950. The Canadian documents exposed the top-secret UFO group, the MJ-12. Some ex-government scientists gave testimony that this group did in fact exist.

Theorists argue that if a fraction of the documents are real, and that MJ-12 was set up at the highest level of government in the Pentagon, then something inexplicable really did happen at Roswell. Something that was going to threaten national security and even perhaps the safety of Earth.

Denial of Eyewitness Accounts

Government and mainstream media conspire to make sure that UFO sightings are not taken seriously. They replace eyewitness explanations with more 'probable' ones, like swamp gases, light aberrations, atmospheric phenomena, weather balloons, misidentified aircraft, and hoaxes. For example, in January of 2008 dozens of witnesses reported seeing a UFO in Stephenville, Texas. Despite compelling witness accounts, the military discounted the event, pointing to 'optical illusions' and 'superior mirages'.

Major UFO Mass Sightings From Around the World

UFOs are a global phenomenon, with known UFO hotspots on every continent. The US has the highest number of recorded UFO sightings of any country in the world and Mexico follows closely. Canada and Australia also have a large number of reported UFO sightings. Why are these countries the preferred destination for our alien visitors? It has been suggested that when sightings are encouraged to be reported, the public share their experiences.

UFO research reveals that a UFO sighting occurs somewhere on the Earth every three minutes! While most of the UFO sightings witnessed by individual persons are dismissed as some confusion or delusion, it is difficult to disregard the sightings that occur in public places and are witnessed by a large number of people.

One of the most dramatic, mass UFO sightings was in Los Angeles, in 1942. It became known as the famous Battle of Los Angeles and, no, once again it was not the title of a Hollywood movie!

Battle of Los Angeles

In the early hours of 25 February 1942, the sound of air-raid sirens and anti-aircraft fire shattered the peaceful sleep of local Los Angeles residents. Naturally, the first thought in their minds was that another wave of Japanese planes was attacking America on its own soil. Only weeks after Pearl Harbor the country was not prepared for another surprise attack.

High-pitched warnings and continuous rounds of artillery firings illuminated the sky as volunteer air-raid wardens headed to the streets, which were in total blackout. Searchlight beams crisscrossed the blackened skies, looking for attacking aircraft. Would their light reveal enemy planes?

A surreal, giant glowing object moved slowly above suburban Los Angeles. The 37th Coast Artillery Brigade began firing anti-aircraft shells at 3.08 a.m. in a 30-minute barrage, sending fragmented artillery shells flying over homes and businesses. It was reported that approximately 1,400 rounds of ammunition were fired at the giant UFO, yet it appeared indestructible. Strangely, the anti-aircraft shells seemed to hit nothing. Despite the intense barrage, no aircraft wreckage was ever recovered.

The object eventually made its way over Long Beach, before it silently disappeared from view. The cannons were now silent.

At 7.21 a.m. the siren gave the all-clear and citizens could finally breathe a sigh of relief. They'd survived the attack. But what exactly had they survived? Who or what had attacked?

The aftermath

Initially there were reports cited of witnesses seeing formations of war planes overhead as a result of dogfights between enemy and US fighter planes.

Newspaper reports were scarce. Government and military officials often gave conflicting statements to the press about what happened. The military stated that no US aircraft were in the air, and there was no evidence of enemy planes. The raid was simply a false alarm. Many people weren't convinced. They believed the aircraft they'd seen was extra-terrestrial. The government was accused of orchestrating a cover-up.

LA Times photo showing an ominous saucer-like object hovering over the city.

The War Department report stated that the unidentified flying objects were Japanese. This, of course, was denied by the Japanese at the end of World War II. Had it not been for the war, news of this event might have gained more publicity.

To this day, no one knows for sure what flew over Los Angeles that night and how it evaded the city's air defences.

Famous UFO Sightings That Shocked Witnesses

The Aurora Texas UFO Crash, 1897 – A pilot or an alien?

On 17 April 1897, a mysterious loud noise woke the sleepy town of Aurora, Texas. It was coming from an unidentified aircraft that had appeared out of nowhere and crashed into a windmill. The debris of the plane was spread over several acres and the body of the pilot was badly disfigured. Reports from witnesses claim that, despite his extensive injuries, he did not resemble a human being.

Stadio Artemio Franchi, Florence, Italy, 1954 – What lurks behind the bright lights?

On 27 October 1954, in a sports stadium that held around 10,000 fans, something extraordinary happened. The stadium was flooded with dazzling lights, seemingly out of nowhere. People reported that the lights were cigar-shaped and not like anything they'd ever seen before.

Kecksburg, USA, 1965 – A meteor or something else?

The UFO crash near the small village of Kecksburg and was witnessed by thousands in the US and Canada. The object was described as being about the size of a small car, shaped like an acorn and decorated with hieroglyphics.

The crash was so intense that it caused sonic booms and dropped hot metal debris, starting grass fires in Michigan and Ohio. The military reportedly found nothing in the woods, except for signs of meteor damage. However, locals have claimed that a large object was recovered and taken away on the back of a truck.

The Phoenix Lights, USA, 1997 – Flares or alien lights?

Five lights in a triangle formation were first seen above Henderson, Nevada, on 13 March 1997. More sightings followed as the lights made their way to Phoenix, Arizona, where literally thousands of people witnessed the phenomenon. The US government issued an official explanation for the Phoenix lights, stating that they were flares dropped by US aircraft. This explanation was never taken seriously by those who witnessed the event.

Guadalajara, Mexico, 2004 – Birds, helium balloons or alien craft?

Guadalajara holds the record for the highest number of reported UFO sightings in Mexico. In June 2004, it was also host to the largest concentration of UFOs ever sighted. A swarm of bright lights gathered over the city and hung around for several hours. No explanation was given for this phenomenon, however witnesses and UFO experts rule out birds or helium balloons, which leaves only one other probable explanation.

Nazi Alien Contact

In 1937, ten years before Roswell, it is claimed that alien spacecraft crashed into German territory. Although research into wingless aircraft or flying saucers had been undertaken in Germany years earlier, the crashed alien spacecraft helped to advance propulsion, electronics and design.

According to official documents, the Germans actually created an assembly line to manufacture a flying disc weapon called the Kugelblitz (ball lightning). These radio-controlled craft were made in underground factories in Thuringia. They were manoeuvrable and able to fly at high speeds. More effective was that they emitted a strong electrostatic field to disrupt the instruments and circuits of enemy planes, causing them to malfunction and crash.

Nazi Germany created a number of other super weapons and craft. If they had had more time, they would have used these effectively against the Allies and the outcome of the war might have been very different.

Some of their experimental creations included: Stealth aircraft, imploder vortex motor, remote-controlled flying saucers, V-2 rockets, synthetic fuel, high explosives, advanced aircraft and low-yielding atomic bomb. All this from alien-inspired technology!

Leading scientists in Nazi Germany at the time were also working on anti-gravity and time-travel theories. They were using many resources in an attempt to develop a time machine. Perhaps alien technology accelerated their progress.

Wonder weapon or a time-travel device?

Engineer Viktor Schauberger was the inventor of the revolutionary imploder motor that created an imploding vortex. That motor may have been the basis for the Nazis' incredible secret weapon known as The Bell.

The Bell or 'Die Glocke' is famous for its supposed advanced technology. It was the Nazis' most notorious secret weapon and was constructed in secret near the Czechoslovakian border. Some debate whether it existed at all, however there are details from old documents suggesting that it did.

The Bell is also known as The Nazi Bell and is described as being a device 'made out of a hard, heavy metal', approximately 2.7 metres (9 feet) wide and 3.7 to 4.6 metres (12 to 15 feet) high, having a shape similar to that of a large bell. It had the power of a radiation device when filled with mercury and other liquid metals, but more than that, some believe it could manipulate time and space, including space travel. It was described as a multidimensional motor that neutralised gravity and reportedly created inter-dimensional rifts in space-time.

It seems by all accounts that this was a dangerous machine – with the powerful radiation that was emitted during the experiments causing serious health problems and even the death of scientists and workers on the project. When active, The Bell was said to glow a bluish colour, like the destroyer the *SS Eldridge*, and make strange buzzing noises. It was meant to have the ability to generate wormholes, which then enabled it to transport objects through time and space. How were the Nazis able to build a time machine in the 1930s, designed to warp space-time and allow travel back through time? Did the Nazis create a wormhole and land in some other time? Scientists believe that this is possible.

The Third Reich claimed to have invented this advanced technology, which would normally have taken decades or centuries to perfect, but it is widely believed that they got a little outside help from alien sources.

With all this alien-inspired technology, it was only a matter of time before Nazi Germany believed it could dominate the world ... but time is everything, and the Third Reich ran out of time. The Bell disappeared after the end of World War II, its existence still a mystery.

Kecksburg UFO

Back on 9 December 1965, something very unusual happened in Kecksburg, Pennsylvania, USA, known as The Kecksburg UFO Incident.

Thousands of people saw a large fireball over six American states. The fireball object dropped metal debris along its path. Grass fires sprang up. Witnesses saw the UFO crash into the woods of Kecksburg.

This was no flying saucer. It was an object shaped like an acorn – not unlike the Nazi Bell. Those who saw the event reported that the unidentified flying object eventually crashed into woods of Kecksburg and locals rushed to the scene to take a look.

Once the military arrived, the object was quickly taken away – the official story was that it was no UFO but a meteor.

Was this The Bell that had gone through time and landed over 20 years later in Kecksburg? Not all Nazi scientists were tried at the Nuremberg Trials. Many were relocated to the US after the war and employed by the US government. Could the American government have wanted them to continue further work on time travel? Were they able to bring back The Bell through time?

This is a recreation of what The Nazi Bell may have looked like.

The Philadelphia Experiment

In October 1943, the *SS Eldridge* became part of a military experiment that has been controversial to this day, with so many questions still waiting to be answered.

Consider the stakes: a race to win a world war and the chance to make scientific history with the world's greatest geniuses – Albert Einstein and Nikola Tesla. The Unified Theory Einstein was supposedly working on was based on the nature and behaviour of all matter and energy – and that it was possible to be invisible to the naked eye and also time-travel. It was Einstein who claimed that once you bend light, you also bend time and space. In other words, this experiment was a time-travel experiment and it was officially known as The Rainbow Project.

Unofficially it has become known as the Philadelphia Experiment.

A number of bizarre things happened during the tests:

- A green haze appeared around the boat when the electric cable was wrapped around the hull. The electro-magnetic field increased and began to extend out from the ship in all directions.
- After a blue flash, the destroyer disappeared from sight and supposedly materialised again in a bay in Norfolk, Virginia. After four hours, the ship reappeared in its original location in Philadelphia.

What had happened in that time and how had it affected the crew?

It was bizarre. During the experiment, crew members claimed they were able to walk through solid objects and walls, but not so when they reappeared at Philadelphia. Tragically, some were found embedded or fused into the metal of the ship – their bodies had been trapped within bulkheads, decks and railings. Not all the crew returned.

Of those who did return, a number died soon after, some suffered mental breakdowns, and others mysteriously faded from view and disappeared before people's eyes. At times they materialised again after a few minutes or hours. Some never returned.

UFO hotspots around the world

If you want to experience a UFO sighting, there's a good chance that you will see one or more at these famous world hot spots:

Pacific Coast Highway, California, US

Fancy a long drive with strange lights to keep you company? The stretch between San Diego and San Francisco is one spot people have claimed to have sighted UFOs regularly since 1947.

Nullarbor Plain, Australia

This remote area in the Australian outback has been a UFO hotspot ever since the 1950s when the British military started atomic bombing in the area. Many people travelling across the barren Nullarbor Plain have reported being chased by UFOs. It's also a popular place for alien abduction.

Warminster, England

Numerous sightings and sounds have been reported since the 1960s. Many enthusiasts camping above Cradle Hill watch for UFOs. Strange humming noises, tremors, lights, crop circles, UFOs, and even alien abductions are all part of this town's history – and mysterious Stonehenge is not far away.

Extra-terrestrial Highway, Nevada, US

Route 375 was officially named Extra-terrestrial Highway in 1996 after several claims of UFO sightings along this route. What makes it even more of a hotspot is that the highway passes through Area 51 – the secret US Air Force base where the alleged UFO craft that crashed in Roswell is meant to be stored.

Bonnybridge, Scotland

Up to 300 UFO sightings are reported every year in Bonnybridge and surrounding areas. It is highly likely, therefore, that you may have a UFO experience in this part of the world, and perhaps visit Loch Ness, home of the mysterious Loch Ness monster.

Phoenix, Arizona, US

It may be that Phoenix is close to Area 51 as well as its proximity to the suspected alien base, Dulce, New Mexico, that puts Arizona on top of the list for UFO sightings.

San Clemente, Chile

There have been such a high number of UFO sightings in the small town of San Clemente, nestled in the Andes Mountains, that in 2008 a new trail called The UFO Trail was opened. Locals say that this 19-mile (30.5 kilometres) stretch is a favourite landing spot for alien spacecraft.

Mexico City, Mexico

Home to one of the largest mass UFO sightings in 1991, many eyewitnesses claimed to have seen a strange aircraft hovering in the sky during a solar eclipse. In March 2015, a webcam captured footage of a supposed UFO near the Colima volcano.

Istanbul, Turkey

In 2008, a night guard recorded several UFOs on video over a period of four months. The Sirius UFO Space Science Research Centre called the footage the 'most important images of a UFO ever filmed'.

Sochi, Russia

This coastal city by the Black Sea is known for its strange sightings – luminous objects and flying saucers. Conspiracy theorists suggest that Bytkha Mountain has a UFO base where a stargate has been used for alien travel.

Colares Island, Brazil

This perfect holiday destination has a mysterious background. In 1977, an outbreak of UFO sightings took place on the island, which today is referred to as the Colares Flap. Two people died and over a hundred were injured when powerful laser-like beams were fired from bright flying objects. The light beams left tiny holes in witnesses' skin, which eventually turned to scars. Though the government ordered an investigation, the results were not made public. Residents in this area continue to sight UFOs to this day, but most sightings don't make the news.

Manitoba, Canada

There's pretty much every type of UFO sighted at this hotspot in Canada. According to witnesses, triangles, chevrons, boomerangs, orbs, fireballs, spheres and saucer-shaped craft have recently been seen in this area over Canada. One of the most famed mass UFO sighting cases occurred here in 1975–76. It was known as the Charlie Redstar Flap.

The M Triangle, Russia

Located in the Ural Mountains, the M Triangle is Russia's most popular UFO spot. There have been numerous reports of strange lights, flying craft, unusual symbols in the sky, and encounters with translucent beings

UFOs in space

More than a dozen American and Russian space travellers have spoken openly about encountering UFOs during their missions, yet NASA and its Russian equivalent are not giving the public any information.

Shuttle astronauts and Russian cosmonauts witnessed UFOs during Gemini orbital missions, as well as en route to the moon.

Interestingly, now that NASA has rovers on Mars and we have new technology that allows us to scan its reports of UFOs, sightings have increased outside of Earth.

UFOs could be anything from extra-terrestrials to a military operation testing out some new technology. With reported sightings more regular than ever, is it because there is actually more activity going on? Or is the increase in UFO reports exaggerated? Some of these UFO reports can be debunked as fakes, however some video footage makes it difficult to deny that there is 'something out there' that is not of earthly nature.

Part 3

The Aliens Are Here

Up the airy mountain,
Down the rushy glen,
We daren't go a-hunting
For fear of little men.

— William Allingham, 1824-1889

Do you believe in extra-terrestrial intelligence? What about the idea that, not only do they exist, but that they are currently in contact with the Earth?

Abductees, military personnel, whistleblowers, even reputable scientists, have been thoroughly tested by a vast range of neurologists, hypnotists, psychologists, etc., proving undisputedly that these people have had contact with ETs. This contacted is reported to be both positive and negative. Some of these beings may appear odd or paranormal in nature to us due to their level of intelligence and the way they interact with reality, which is difficult for us to understand.

In the past, when investigating UFO and alien sightings, it became apparent that there was a need for a structured system for everyone to use. One of the most well-known systems is still the Hynek System, named after astronomer and astrophysicist Dr Joseph Allen Hynek, who worked with the US Air Force researching UFOs, including the research for Project Blue Book.

UFO Sighting Reports Classifications

The least invasive encounter is a Close Encounter of the First Kind (CE1) – the sighting of a UFO within a 150 metres range or less.

A Close Encounter of the Second Kind (CE2) is a sighting of a UFO that leaves some form of physical evidence behind, such as broken glass, radiation, scorching or an unknown substance.

The next encounter was made popular by Stephen Spielberg's movie, *Close Encounters of the Third Kind.* A CE3 is a visual sighting of an occupant or entity associated with a UFO. In other words, observing an extra-terrestrial being.

A Close Encounter of the Fourth Kind (CE4) is an abduction of an individual by an alien being or race.

A Close Encounter of the Fifth Kind (CE5) is a direct contact or communication with an alien being or race. Those who experience this contact sometimes call themselves 'channellers'. They claim to have messages from the alien groups for the human race.

There are lesser-known encounters that are not officially part of Hynek's classification system:

A Close Encounter of the Sixth Kind involves the death of a human or animal associated with a UFO sighting. There have been cases of cattle mutilations attributed to UFO interference.

A Close Encounter of the Seventh Kind is the creation of a human/alien hybrid, either by sexual reproduction or artificial methods. A hybrid is the genetically manipulated product of alien and human DNA.

Alien Communication

It happened to Agent Scully, the character on the TV show *The X-Files*, but real people all over the world have claimed it has happened to them. Agent Scully of *The X-Files* was abducted by aliens, experimented on, and later had a hybrid child. One could argue that this story is fiction, however the plot used by the producers was taken from case studies of people – real people whose stories made it to the news.

Reports of alien abductions began in the 1940s – around the time of Roswell. A coincidence? It's been a mystery and psychiatrists have looked at years of data to explain this phenomenon. The official line is that the majority of psychologists say that abductions are in fact lucid dreams.

The theory, now, is that because we no longer fear demons and sexual repression, alien encounters and abductions have replaced these outdated fears, which means that they are all hallucinations produced by a panic-stricken brain.

The fact is that abductions are reported all over the world, in large cities and rural areas, any time of day or night, and have happened to many individuals, regardless of their race, social status, religious belief or political persuasion. The other vital piece of the puzzle is this: how do you explain physical illnesses and injuries after a reported abduction that took place in the open and not in the victim's home during sleep time?

Disturbingly, abductees report that they were taken against their will for medical testing or for sexual reproduction procedures. Many such encounters are described as terrifying or humiliating, yet some describe them as transformative. Alien beings most associated with conducting these experiments are known as the 'greys' – short, grey-skinned humanoids with large, pear-shaped heads, large black eyes, tiny noses and slits for mouths.

Many abductions are not reported because the abductees fear ridicule from medical authorities and other people. Do they want to risk being labelled mentally unstable or psychotic? Not likely. Can all these people be making it up? Is it a collective hallucination? And if that were the case, why? Could extra-terrestrial life be confused with paranormal creatures and ghosts? Could these people be entering stargates to different dimensions, rather than being visited here on earth? The answer is that we simply don't know.

There are therapists who deal with abductees and their traumatic experiences for those brave enough to seek help. Most abductees are normal people just like you and me. What they experience may look like this:

At first it's just a strange light ...

Imagine a regular drive in your car. You see a light following close behind you. You may decide to pull over to the side of road – it may not be your decision, but that's what you do. The light is no longer behind you. Now it's above you. And it's coming closer towards you. Only, it's no longer just a light. It's a craft – a spaceship. And it has strange beings in it that you can see ...

There's someone in your room ...

You may be at home and you can't be sure that you're not dreaming, but there is an alien or two walking through your bedroom wall, door or window. You are paralysed and can't speak. They lead you out, making you 'float' outside to where their spaceship is waiting to beam you up.

They've got you captured ...

You are inside a spaceship in a room that looks like a doctor's examination room or a dentist's room. The alien beings, or greys, remove your clothing and lay you down on a hard metal table.

You can expect a lot of prodding. Parts of your body, especially your head and genitals, are examined with various instruments. It is not a pleasant experience.

You have tiny implants placed in your body to track you. These are not as bad as the strange physical markings on your body you will notice later on.

There is usually some form of telepathic communication. You are told one or more of these things: that they are from a distant galaxy and their planet is dying; that mankind is about to self-destruct; that they need your eggs or sperm to propagate their race or create a hybrid one.

You are then shown rooms containing other humans, or nurseries full of babies, and told that one or more are yours!

You're never the same again ...

You usually find yourself back where you were when the aliens first visited you. It is likely there will be missing time.

In fact, you can be sure you've lost more than an hour of your life or more.

Your memory will be affected – you won't remember where you've been or what's happened to you, until some time later when you start to fill in some blanks. If your memory still won't budge, it's time to go under hypnosis and then you relive your nightmare all over again.

You are not alone in this ...

It's a scary thing for any of these scenarios to happen. But countless people in many countries have reported being abducted by aliens and have experienced what's just been described. It seems rather odd that with so many similar experiences, there hasn't been a credible explanation that's satisfied the scientific community and the more open-minded individuals. Although many alien abductions go unreported, these ones made it in the news. Some even had front-page coverage!

Case Studies of Alien Abductions

A Fishing Trip Gone Wrong:
The Allagash Waterway Abduction, Maine, US, 1976

Four friends were on a fishing trip, determined to catch the 'one that got away'. It didn't matter it was dark. There was nothing better than a lil' night-time fishin'.

Jack and Jim Weiner, and friends Chuck Rak and Charlie Foltz, built a large fire on the banks of Eagle Lake and were in their canoes on the lake when they noticed a very bright object in the sky.

The object began to change colour and one of the men used a flashlight to signal to it. The object began to move towards them. What was it? They were in the middle of a lake and a light was shining on them. They began to frantically paddle towards shore.

It was too late – the UFO moved above closer. The next thing they knew they were sitting on the shore and the large fire they 'thought' they had just started had burned out completely into a pile of cold ash. There had clearly been a series of time lapses. How long had they been gone and where had they been?

The men returned home, disturbed by their experience. Predictably, all four were haunted by nightmares in which they remembered being experimented on by aliens in a spacecraft. Under regressive hypnosis, it was determined that all four of the men had been abducted and subjected to humiliating and invasive testing, including the extraction of semen and other bodily fluids.

All four men received separate hypnosis sessions, but their stories were exactly the same. Since they were also artists, they were able to draw startlingly accurate pictures of the exam room, the aliens, and the instruments the aliens used on them. They also passed lie-detector tests, verifying that they were telling the truth.

Five Hopping Creatures Out of this World: 25 January 1967, Massachusetts, US

Imagine seeing five creatures 'hopping' towards your house and straight through your solid wood door and instantly putting your entire family into a trance.

That's what happened to Betty Andreasson and her family. The aliens were described by Betty and her father as being short and without usual human characteristics, and one of them was clearly the leader. They communicated only telepathically, and Betty felt calm and unconcerned even while everyone but she and her father were in a state of suspended animation.

Betty was then taken aboard a spacecraft and was subjected to invasive (and sometimes painful) examinations. Roughly four hours later, Betty was returned to her family and the aliens released them all from their trance and hypnotised Betty so that she would forget much about her time on the mother ship.

Eight years later, still plagued by the vague memories of her experience, Betty underwent twelve months of extensive psychiatric evaluations and a number of psychological and medical tests, including regressive hypnosis and polygraphs. After all was said and done, it was determined that Betty was sane and believed everything about her very vivid alien abduction experience. Her case is one of the most famous UFO abduction cases to date.

Lights on the Moors:
1987, Ilkley Moor, Yorkshire, UK

There had been mysterious lights in the moors of Yorkshire in England and policeman Philip Spencer was hoping to take some photographs with his camera to try and solve the mystery. The moors are mysterious and spooky at the best of times, but the lights added another level of eeriness.

Using a compass to lead the way, Spencer was moving through the dense fog when he saw a small, strange creature that seemed to be trying to 'wave him away'. Spencer raised his camera and got one shot before the creature turned and ran away.

Ever the policeman, Spencer gave chase. Nothing could have prepared him for what he witnessed: a large UFO lifting off from the moor nearby. He rushed to the village to get his film exposed, and it was then that he noticed that an hour of his life was missing – his watch had stopped, and his compass was pointing south when it should have been pointing north.

The Alien Abduction That Became
a Best-selling Novel:
26 December 1985, upstate New York

This really does sound like a chilling story from a bestseller. A remote cabin in the woods. Woken by a strange creature in the middle of the night. Coming to in the woods, freezing cold, hours later with no memory of what happened. That's the story of author Whitley Strieber, who went on to write about his alien abduction experiences in his novel, *Communion*.

It was only under hypnosis that he recovered his memories of being taken into a spacecraft. One particular horrifying memory was that of having his brain probed – one of the experiments that had been performed on him. He described one of the aliens as a typical-looking grey:

> 'I saw two dark holes for eyes and a black down-turning line of a mouth. My memory … is of a tiny, squat person, crouching as it huddled over something. He had been given a box and now slid it open, revealing an extremely shiny, hair-thin needle mounted on a black surface.
>
> This needle glittered when I saw it out of the corner of my eye, but was practically invisible straight on.
>
> I became aware – I think I was told – that they proposed to insert this into my brain. If I had been afraid before, I now became quite simply crazed with terror.'

He's always claimed that these were real events. Polygraph tests showed that he was being truthful in describing his alien encounter. Other brain abnormalities were ruled out by MRI. He was tested for temporal lobe epilepsy, a condition that causes vivid hallucinations, but there was no evidence of him having this disease.

Critics and debunkers continue to try and discredit Whitley Strieber's abduction story, as it has had the most public exposure and is written more like science fiction than a biography.

So Famous That The X-Files Re-enacted This Australian Abduction: Belgrave, Australia, August 1993

This story begins like a Stephen King horror. But what happened to Kelly Cahill on this dark, wintry night was beyond a nightmare – it was much worse. It was real.

Kelly Cahill was driving home with her husband when a craft flew overhead – a plane maybe. But then Kelly thought she saw a bright blimp and, as their car neared closer to the brightness, the lights from the craft began to separate into a row of round, orange lights.

She recalled that there were silhouettes standing in these orange circles that looked like people.

The craft then flew away from the field where it had landed and Kelly said that further down the road they saw another bright light like a wall across the road. It was blinding, but relaxing. When she and her husband gained consciousness, they were still on the road driving home, but they'd lost an hour.

But that wasn't the worst of it. Kelly discovered a strange triangular mark near her navel and a small cut on her bikini line, similar to a laparoscopy mark. She was unwell for the next two weeks and rushed to hospital for intense stomach pains and unexplained bleeding.

It may have been the pain that reawakened her memories of being abducted that night. She remembered getting out of the car and walking towards the craft. Dark beings approached her. The UFO was around 150 feet (45.7 metres) in diameter and very tall aliens had gathered underneath it.

> 'This energy went through me … It was a low-level frequency that came in waves, so dense I could physically feel it. That absolutely terrified me. I can't explain the horror I felt and I just began screaming, and the minute I did, the eyes on these things lit up and they came charging across the field.'

Horrified, Kelly recalled being lifted off her feet and thrown back where she couldn't see anything.

Another family backed up Kelly's story by claiming that they, too, had seen the aliens, lost a big span of time, and that they recalled being subjected to invasive medical examinations on a spacecraft.

To this day, there has been no plausible explanation for what happened to Kelly and her husband that night. Or why. Except if we take it at face value for what it is – an alien abduction.

Fermi's Paradox

If there have been abductions as an extreme form of communication, why have we not already communicated with alien life in space with our sophisticated communications and presumably the aliens' advanced knowledge of technologies?

Fermi's Paradox also addresses this very same question. This term was created by physicists Enrico Fermi and Michael Hart, who revealed this contradiction: the high probability estimates for alien life in space and the lack of evidence for such alien civilisations. Based on these arguments, it's possible that many aliens should have invented interstellar travel, which means that UFO sightings on Earth should not just be limited to conspiracy theorists but could occur to everyone.

Edward Snowden, famous for leaking top-secret information about NSA (National Security Agency) surveillance activities in 2013, believes that if alien existence cannot be proved, then encryption is the reason – that we can't understand what aliens might be saying because their communication sounds like noise to us. It's encrypted for obvious reasons – security. Snowden believes that if any intelligent species from another planet existed, then they would use encryption by default, and it's possible we have already heard from alien life in space, yet not realised it:

> 'So what we're hearing – which is actually an alien television show or a phone call or a message between their planet and their own GPS constellation, whatever it happens to be – is indistinguishable to us from cosmic microwave background radiation.'

Aliens, Leprechauns and Fairies

It can be assumed that anyone not obviously human in nature must be an extra-terrestrial. Could today's aliens be the fairies and demons of yesteryear? Gnomes, demons, leprechauns, pixies, fairies, pookas, shapeshifters, angels, Big Foot or Yeti, and other exotic creatures would then certainly fit in this category. The space creatures in the movie *Star Wars* are perfect examples of the diversity of alien creatures. Fictional character Chewbacca, also known as Chewie, is a Big Foot lookalike. He's a wookie, an intelligent, tall, hairy being from the planet Kashyyk and loyal friend and co-pilot on Han Solo's craft, The Millennium Falcon.

Many children have 'invisible friends' who can take on the shape of fairies, as do some adults who claim to see

fairies and orbs. Jean Hingley had an eerie experience when
she saw strange little creatures in her house in England in
1979. Unlike other alien encounter stories, these small beings
(1 to 1.2 metres in height) had wings, were covered in silvery
green, had pointed caps and glowed with a brilliant rainbow
light and floated above the floor. There may be a case for the
theory that today's alien visitors are the space-age equivalent
of fairies and other magical creatures in our fairytales.

The Aliens Have Landed

There are many of us who ask the question: why do alien
species want to communicate with us? We know from
reports about cattle mutilations, suspected of being carried
out by alien beings, that it may have something to do with
genetic experiments. Alien species of differing origins have
attempted to crossbreed our genes, requiring an upgrade of
their existence. They have sought and targeted our genetic
pool for saving their race. This has been going on since
early in our history with the Anunnaki carrying out genetic
testing and breeding, mineral mining, and slavery for known
and unknown purposes.

Numerous extra-terrestrials or star beings have played
an integral role in the history of Earth and its inhabitants.
Generally it has been beneficial for the planet, solar system
and beyond. Aliens interacting with Earth have origins in
constellations from Lyra, Vega, Zeta Reticuli, Arcturus,

Sirius, Orion, Pleiades and neighbouring galaxies such as Andromeda.

As much as these extra-terrestrials have given us vast amounts of information for our advancement, we have also been denied information about deadly new technologies that have proved to be a risk to not just our planet but also our universe. If we are to believe the many stories from abductees, these superior races have also exploited us.

What seems to be most disturbing is that our government agencies today and the ruling elite of the past have had knowledge of these practices and sanctioned them with secret deals and cover-ups.

Conversely, benevolent alien beings also want to protect us and teach us how to look after our Earth. There have been unofficial reports of aliens warning us not to destroy ourselves during the last World Wars.

It's estimated that there are over one hundred or more known types of aliens that have visited Earth and continue to do so at the present time.

Alien Species

The Greys

The most common types of aliens seen are the Greys, and they are certainly no allies to Earth. These are the typical aliens seen in movies and described in alien abduction

stories. They are about 4 feet tall (1.2 metres), have grey
skin, with an oversized head, large slanted eyes, small nose
and a tiny slit for a mouth. They seldom speak, as most
communication is carried out telepathically. There are
subspecies of Greys – the Rigelians from the Rigel star
system and the Zeta Reticuli from the constellation Orion
and the star system Zeta Reticuli.

According to UFOlogists, there are not as many of
these Greys as we are led to believe. They have a number
of clones among them. The Greys are responsible for the
majority of abductions and it is speculated that a pact has
been made between government agencies and this group
of aliens. It has been suggested that humans have received

advanced alien technology in return for the abduction of humans and experimentation. The Greys are claimed to be responsible for cattle mutilations, genetic manipulation and impregnating human females and later extracting foetuses.

Interestingly, it is said they have been cloning themselves due to radioactive nuclear exposure that is causing a decline in reproduction, and each time they re-clone the genetic copy becomes weaker. They are no friends of humans, regarding us as an inferior civilisation, but with the necessary DNA for their experimentation – and survival.

The Tall Greys are between 7 to 8 feet tall (2.1 to 2.4 metres), hairless and pale and are known as ambassadors between humans and aliens. They supervise abductions and human experiments but are not present during these events. Those tasks are left to the genetically engineered worker race, the shorter Greys. Their mission is to develop a stable human Grey hybrid race to save them from extinction.

The Nordics

The Nordics are also called Blondes and Swedes and display very similar characteristics to the Nordic people of Scandinavia. They are said to be tall humanoids 6 to 7 feet (1.8 to 2.1 metres) with blond hair, fair or dark skin, mostly with blue eyes and mostly male. Another feature is their tight clothing – usually a one-piece jumpsuit.

Contacts from Nordics were at their height in the 1950s to '60s, where contactees claimed to have witnessed the Nordics beaming down from either metallic crescent-shaped spaceships or large cigar-shaped ones. They were known back then as Space Brothers.

These aliens have been considered benevolent and magical beings, communicating with humans about taking care of the Earth's environment and world peace. Some UFOlogists believe that the Nordics warn humans about the Greys and their experiments, however others claim that Nordics have been seen in the same spaceships as Greys and therefore cannot be trusted. Their role is not always clear-cut.

Researchers speculate that US President Dwight D. Eisenhower met with Nordic aliens at Edwards Air Force Base in February 1954. It was to negotiate an agreement over technology exchange and the elimination of the

American nuclear arsenal. Probable? Conspiracy theorists would think so. However, as is expected, these claims have been dismissed as untrue and fabricated.

Pleiadeans

The Plciades star cluster is a tiny, misty dipper of stars also known as M45 or the Seven Sisters – it consists of seven stars, and is in the constellation of Taurus. You can see the Pleiades from anywhere in the world.

In both myth and science, the Pleiades are considered to be sibling stars. Astronomers tell us that the Pleiades stars were born from the same cloud of gas and dust around 100 million years ago, which makes them approximately 430 light years away.

From this star cluster come the Pleiadeans – a group of alien beings, either blond, Nordic humanoids or brunettes, who were once colonised by the Lyrans and then invaded by a reptilian race from Alpha-Draconis.

Indigenous people from all around the world are familiar with this alien species, as they are known to have made contact during our early history, as well as during the tumultuous world wars. The Native American Indian people, the Hopis, called the Pleiadeans the 'Chuhukon', meaning those who cling together. They considered themselves direct descendants of the Pleiadeans.

What is the role of the Pleiadeans on Earth? Apparently the Pleiadeans were the first humanoid society to develop hyper space travel and have been sharing that knowledge with Earth's government agencies for a number of years. Their superior technology in our hands is supposedly supervised by them, so that we don't end up destroying humankind.

Lyrans

Beings from the Lyran constellation, known as Lyrans, were the original ancestors of humanity's galactic family. It's believed that their civilisation reached a very high technological level, but due to factions and wars, much of their society was destroyed.

This led them to escape to and colonise the Pleiades, the Hyades (Taurus constellation) and Vega, which is also in Lyra.

The Lyrans are considered important because they came to visit Earth during the time of Lemuria and Atlantis. They contributed advanced knowledge and technology which later civilisations, such as the Sumerians, the Egyptians and the Mayans, benefited from.

Men In Black (MIBs)

They wear dark suits and sunglasses and drive black cars. They have pale skin and their eyes are sensitive to light. If that's not scary enough, they are intimidating if you find yourself meeting these beings at a UFO scene. They're here for one reason – to keep witnesses silent about what they've seen.

They are the equivalent of secret government organisations – only from another galaxy.

Are they controlled by other species like the Greys or a reptilian race? Are they human, humanoid or artificial intelligence? Are they hired by our government agencies or are they impersonating these authorities?

It's mysterious how Men in Black suddenly appear and then drive away – where do they go? They've been spotted disappearing into mountains, canyons or tunnels and in some cases just vanishing into thin air. Some believe there is a good chance they may live in some sort of complex underground system.

Arcturians

The Arcturians are from Arcturus – Arcturus is the brightest star in the Bootes constellation, which is thirty-six light years from earth.

The most ancient race of our entire Milky Way Galaxy, the Arcturians are a highly evolved race of alien beings. They are profoundly aware, innovative and experienced. These beings are the most sophisticated and intelligent group in the universe, often referred to as 'elders'. They travel the universe in their high-tech starships and are reportedly respected by other alien life forms for their advanced knowledge in education, medicine, telepathic communication, teleportation, time travel and more.

They are regarded by some as a fifth-dimension civilisation – an idyllic future Earth. All this is good news for humans. The Arcturians are on our side and are committed to keeping us safe, overseeing evolutionary processes of life here and deterring military and government from potentially annihilating the planet through war or chemical warfare.

You'd expect the Arcturians to be imposing-looking beings, but they are quite ordinary – short at 3-4 feet (1 to 1.2 metres) in height, slender with greenish skin, dark, large, almond-shaped eyes and only three fingers. Among other things, Arcturians are both telepathic and telekinetic (able to move objects with their minds). They do live a long life of 350 to 400 years on average, due to their ability to transcend time and space. Other than spacecraft, the Arcturians are said to have bases on Earth, mostly inside of mountains, and on the moon.

Sirians

Sirius is the celebrity constellation due to the fact that just about every civilisation on Earth mentions it in their records. Sirians are from the Sirius star system, known as the Dog Star constellation of Canis Major, 8.6 light years from Earth. What makes Sirius so special? Is it because it is the brightest star in the sky? Or is it also because we have an ancient and mysterious connection with it?

They are said to be our Father Race who came together to help create humans genetically. Many ancient prophecies and spiritual texts tell us that extra-terrestrials were involved in the creation of human beings. In ancient Egypt Sirius was regarded as the most important star in the sky and most Egyptian gods were associated with the star. Anubis, the dog-headed god of death, had an obvious connection with the Dog Star, but more than that, it's believed that the Great Pyramid of Giza was built in perfect alignment with Sirius.

It was believed to have been the Sirians who gave the Egyptians the help they needed to build the Great Pyramids. It's speculated they were able to transport and lift the huge stones needed to construct pyramids with anti-gravity technology.

The entire process meant that the stone would be weightless and easily moved up or down or from side to side. Instead of taking 40 years to construct the pyramids, it could have taken as little as six months.

It wasn't just the Egyptians who worshipped Sirius. The star's celestial movement was also observed and revered by ancient Greeks, Sumerians, Babylonians and many other civilisations. In Chinese and Japanese astronomy, Sirius is known as the 'star of the celestial wolf'. In Native American tribes, it's referred to as 'a dog that follows mountain sheep' or 'wolf star', 'coyote star' and 'dog face'. The Mayans gained their wisdom from the Sirians, as did the Dogon tribe in West Africa. Even the surviving Atlanteans were said to have been rescued by Sirians during the cataclysmic event that sunk Atlantis.

Since our earliest civilisations, the Dog Star has been associated with divinity and is regarded as a source of knowledge and power. Although they were more involved during our planet's past, nowadays the Sirians are more active in time-travel experimentation.

Alpha-Draconians/Draconians

This is the nastiest alien group of all – a corrupt and brutal race that infiltrated our human society thousands of years ago and is the oldest reptilian race in the galaxy.

They are terrifying at 14 to 22 feet tall (4.2 to 6.7 metres) and very muscular. As the name suggests, they look very much like dragons with scales, powerful tails and wings. Draconians have conquered many other worlds and seeded the less fearsome reptilian races. Originally based in the constellation of Orion, approximately 1,400 light years away from Earth, they were part of the 'fallen ones' – a rebellious group that challenged the universal council, not dissimilar to the dark forces in the movie *Star Wars*. It seems that these frightening aliens are using our planet as a supply depot and for biological materials (people and cattle mutilations).

Contactees have described Draconians as being 'extremely clairvoyant, clever, and sinister'.

This should not give us cause for concern, however, as there have not been noted sightings of these extra-terrestrials – Draconians have not been mentioned in recent times. Dragon stories in fantasy novels, however, make sure their presence never leaves our psyche and keeps our survival instincts sharp.

Reptilians or Reptoids

The Reptilians are marginally less destructive and negative than the Draconians, despite the fact that they were seeded by the Draconians. These extra-terrestrials are less confronting due to the fact that they are human in shape and size because they are native to Earth. However, there are obvious characteristics that set them apart from the rest of us – scaly, waterproof skin, three long fingers and a thumb and large eyes with a vertical pupil.

What is known about this alien race is that they were originally left behind by the Alpha-Draconians to colonise Earth. So they've been around for a very long time – and some virtually look like normal humans with Reptilian DNA. The most dangerous aspect of the Reptilians is that they have infiltrated almost all aspects of human life and hold positions of power. They want one thing – power and control – and they do this by manipulating and ruling our major institutions and organisations, including religious, financial, government, military, media and all corporations.

It's interesting to note our universally shared fear of snakes. It makes you wonder if this fear, and often phobia, is part of our shared ancestral-memory DNA to protect us from this dangerous alien race.

Essassani

It's hard to imagine the concept of human hybrids, but after all the stories we hear of alien abductions, experimentation and genetic manipulation from way back in the days of the Sumerian civilisation and the Anunnaki alien beings, it's not surprising there is now a new group. They are called the Essassani.

The Essassani are our Reptilian, Grey-human hybrid relatives. They look Eurasian (European–Asian) with very large eyes, small in height at 5 feet (1.5 metres) with white-grey skin. Females usually have white hair, while the males have no hair.

When the first lot of Greys came to Earth, they had genetically mutated themselves to the point of not being able to reproduce anymore. They could only survive through cloning – which they did, with human DNA. In the past we shared our human genetics with them. Since then a new breed of beings have been created, which are far more advanced than us. Also from the Orion constellation, the Essassani are our contact ambassadors and it is believed that an extra-terrestrial named Basher is channelling information from the Essassani to help us become more highly evolved beings.

Space Police – The Ashtar Command

The Ashtar Command is much like the space police and they make sure order is kept in the galaxy, in particular between six planets in the Orion System – the Deros – which are always in need of their attention.

In fact, this group is so serious about keeping order and control that they even managed to contact us on Earth by overriding the ITN news in southern Britain on 26 November 1977.

It was like any other television news broadcast until a strange buzzing noise interrupted newscaster Ivor Mills as he read out the day's news. Only the audio was affected. Listeners could hardly believe what they heard. It was said to have been a message from someone who claimed to be a representative of the Ashtar Galactic Command.

Interpretations of what was said that night vary, however it was generally agreed that the person speaking called himself Vrillon. This extract from his transcribed speech contains phrases and words that one would expect to see in new-age publications.

'For many years you have seen us as lights in the skies. We speak to you now in peace and wisdom as we have done to your brothers and sisters all over this, your planet Earth.

We come to warn you of the destiny of your race and your world so that you may communicate to your fellow beings the course you must take to avoid the disaster which threatens your world and the beings on our worlds around you.

This is in order that you may share in the great awakening, as the planet passes into the New Age of Aquarius. The New Age can be a time of great peace and evolution for your race, but only if your rulers are made aware of the evil forces that can overshadow their judgments. Be still now and listen, for your chance may not come again.

All your weapons of evil must be removed … You have but a short time to learn to live together in peace and goodwill …'

Imagine the confusion. When the transmission came to an end after five and half minutes, the audio returned as if nothing had happened. Everything went back to normal.

The interference and pulsating noises – gone. The ads came back on loud and annoyingly clear.

Was it a hoax? It would appear that was the general consensus, despite nobody claiming responsibility. Was it the work of a talented hacker? A number of people are convinced that it would have taken someone with superior technical skills to disrupt the network and take over not one, but five transmitters. Was it the work of a genius or was it really an entity named Vrillon from the Ashtar Command – a galactic law enforcer? If so, why haven't we heard from Vrillon or any other extra-terrestrial group since then, in a way that we can understand them?

Ultra Terrestrials – not your normal ET

Suspending disbelief about the existence of extra-terrestrials is difficult for the majority of us. However, it may be a little more acceptable for our rational minds to be open to explanations about other civilisations and mysterious creatures that cohabit this planet with us.

Ultra-terrestrials are like extra-terrestrials, a very technologically and scientifically advanced civilisation except for one major difference: they don't come from space but from Earth. In fact, they have been living among us since the dawn of time. They may be either a different branch of biological evolution, or a certain human culture that, for some reason, evolved much faster than others. Some may look like regular humans – a number of them are strange-looking creatures and beings, ranging from fairies, giants, dwarves and monsters to the exotic, inexplicable and very advanced beings.

Journalist and UFOlogist John Keel used the term 'ultra-terrestrials' to describe UFO occupants he believed to be non-human entities capable of taking on whatever form they want.

Edward Snowden has his own theory about ultra-terrestrials. According to documents which Snowden copied from the CIA, the US government has long known that UFOs exist and that these species are more advanced than us.

The creatures Snowden is referring to are ultra-terrestrials – species that are not alien, but from our Earth, only more advanced. He claims that they've lived here for billions of years and are more developed than us. How does Snowden know this? The CIA stores data-tracking systems and deep-sea sonar, which he has witnessed. The secret status of these systems means that even scientists do not have access to the data. Information about ultra-terrestrials, therefore, is not available to anyone other than those at the top-ranking end of government.

So who are these ultra-terrestrials? Snowden describes them as a type of intelligent homo sapiens who once lived in the Earth's mantle. This is the only place where conditions were more or less stable for billions of years. It's well-known in science that extremophiles can live at different temperatures and these ultra-terrestrials have been able to flourish and develop intelligence at an accelerated pace. Their living conditions in the Earth's mantle have protected their civilisation from the many natural and man-made disasters that have occurred on the surface of the Earth. Not only have they adapted to their conditions, but they have the technology to make their environment habitable.

So far, we humans have been of no interest to ultra-terrestrials, other than keeping an eye on our technology in case it is of future threat to their wellbeing. However, government agencies don't want to take any chances, according to Snowden's leaked documents, and nuclear weapons may protect humans from potential future interference or even attack.

How to Contact ETs

Is there any way we can contact ETs? We can be proactive and contact aliens by getting into the right frame of mind that is ideal for them to pick up our vibrations. These beings have thousands of years of evolution, so things like telepathy, ESP, and psychic transmission are easy for them.

Following these steps will create a favourable potential contact experience:

- Create an exact time each day to meditate.

- Create an invocation to welcome them into your space.
- Meditate.

  In your meditative state, ask a question and see if you get a response.

Alternatively, think only positive thoughts and then look to the skies, expecting to see a UFO – if they pick up your signal through ESP, it may well result in a flashing of their lights or an unexpected appearance on the horizon.

A group who are involved in 'sky watching' for UFOs personally taught this technique to me.

After some Qigong-like poses designed to raise energy levels and focus on energy points in the body, you can meditate by sending out positive messages to star beings in the universe, reassuring them that you are open to communication. This technique helps to raise your vibrations so that sophisticated extra-terrestrials can pick up this signal and are confident in revealing themselves to you.

Mind over matter? It may be simply a state of manifesting what you want to believe, but for sky watchers this is their tried and true method of sighting UFOs at will.

How do you know it's a UFO and not a star? Find the nearest star and watch it for a while. If they move an equal distance, there's a high probability that it's a star too.

Part 4

Unexplained Phenomena

—◦—◦—◯—◉—◦—

'It's time to find out what the truth really is that's out there. We ought to do it, really, because it's right. We ought to do it, quite frankly, because the American people can handle the truth. And we ought to do it because it's the law.'

– John Podesta

Since time began, humans have witnessed and experienced thousands of strange, unexplained phenomena. Many can be explained by science, now, but were misunderstood at the time. But there remain a number that still defy logic, reason and a scientific explanation. They are fascinating and terrifying, but we can't seem to get enough of them. Whether you think any of these stories are real or not, you can't deny that they are immensely interesting and intriguing.

Advanced Astronomy in African Tribe

The Dogon tribe, a farming people in Mali in West Africa, have astronomical knowledge that science has only recently known about. They say that a secret star, Sirius B, orbits its twin, Sirius A. Sirius B is very heavy, invisible, small but powerful – modern science has proved that there is such a star in orbit. Sirius B is totally invisible to the human eye and was photographed for the first time in 1970. How did the Dogon come to have knowledge of this star – knowledge that they have passed down through generations?

They claim they were given this astronomical information (including knowledge of Saturn's rings and the four major moons of Jupiter) from a race of space beings (beings from the sky) that visited Earth from the Sirius star system.

The Dogon also speak of a second star orbiting Sirius – but this is not known yet to our scientists. Maybe it's only a matter of time before we'll know for sure.

The Hopi Indians

Unlike other civilisations around the world who maintain that gods descend from the sky, the Native American Hopi believe the gods came up from the ground. One of the legends references Ant People who inhabit the heart of the

Earth. Artwork displaying the Ant People has an uncanny resemblance to modern Greys, with the large slanted eyes and small grey bodies.

Many of the ancient rock art and carvings depict star charts and drawings that appear to portray extra-terrestrials. The Kachina dance and the spirits they represented may have connections to another planet.

The Hopi Indians believed that the home of the Kachinas was on top of a mountain where there were great cloud formations. It's commonly believed that UFOs often hide in fake lenticular (lens-like) clouds – cloud formations that are supposedly produced to hide their spacecraft. Real lenticular clouds move with the rest of the clouds, whereas these alien-made clouds do not. The spaceships apparently must sit for up to five hours in one place, meaning the clouds are completely still during this time.

Hopi believe aliens (star people) and star knowledge will return at the end of the current cycle of time, as they have in past cycles. According to tradition, their Kachinas (supernatural beings or spirits that are now produced as masked dolls) once visited the Earth to be protected during their world's destruction.

In Hopi and Navajo beliefs, Kachinas are messengers between this world and the next. The doll masks have many designs on them that appear to belong to non-worldly beings.

When the first world was destroyed, people returned to the surface to live as ants for the duration of the second world. The third world describes an advanced civilisation with flying shields and wars between distant cities eventually destroyed by great floods. Sounds familiar? It's not dissimilar to Babylonian mythology and the biblical Great Flood.

The Hopi believe they are the record-keepers – caretakers of the fourth world in exchange for the privilege of living on Earth. The time for the fifth world is near. Hopi prophecy states that 'when the Blue Star Kachina makes its appearance in the heavens, the Fifth World will emerge' and there will be nine signs to foretell this phenomenal event.

> 'In the final days we will look up in our heavens and we will witness the return of the two brothers who helped create this world in the birthing time. Poganghoya is the guardian of our North Pole and his brother Palongawhoya is the guardian of the South Pole.
>
> In the final days the Blue Star Kachina will come to be with his nephews and they will return the Earth to its natural rotation that is counter clockwise. Not far behind the twins will come the Purifier – the Red Kachina, who will bring the Day of Purification. On this day the Earth, her creatures and all life as we know it will change forever.'

The Blue Kachina is usually associated with the planet Sirius, and as for the Red Kachina, we simply don't know.

It seems feasible, however, that the Hopi were prophesying a potential supernova explosion, which will have a direct and disastrous impact on Earth – the equivalent to our end of days or Armageddon. Could this be the heralding of a fifth world? Looking at the world's ecological status and nuclear arms race, it might be worthwhile taking heed of the Hopi's signs.

Sacred Geometry or Alien Information?

Plants bent in peculiar angles; spiralling patterns in wheat fields; bare earth circles; flattened and indented crops. These are known as crop circles. Most of them are found in southern areas of England. They are spectacular intricate geometric patterns that are created in the middle of the night, and virtually impossible to replicate. Science explains it as organised harmonic form, the result of energy interacting with the physical world of plants.

Strangely some circles have been created very quickly, formed in under twenty seconds. Witnesses say that bright coloured orbs or shards of light are seen above the crops during the process. Most designs are circles, circles with rings, patterns and straight lines that create pictograms.

Strange facts about the formation of crops and the surrounding area include the following characteristics:

- The plants are subjected to a short intense burst of heat, which makes the plant bend but not be damaged permanently.
- The composition of the soil around the crop is different from that of the rest of the field. It has been suggested that if water were brought into the formation area, a pattern similar to the crop would also form in the water.

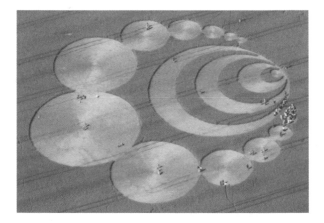

Crop circles are known to alter the local electromagnetic field; often compasses cannot locate north, cameras and mobile phones malfunction, batteries are drained, radio frequencies differ inside the circles, local farm animals avoid the crop circles, car batteries in local towns fail to operate in the morning after one is found in the area.

Are crop circles simply natural phenomena that materialise at crossing points along the Earth's magnetic energy fields? Or are they man-made, as some hoax versions have proved to be?

Many believe that crop circles may well be communications from advanced civilisations beyond our planet, who are contacting us with vital information about the way energy works in the universe. They are showing us new forms of energy that we have always been striving to find – travelling through space-time. Is it a code for new technology? Are they warnings that we are on the verge of destroying our planet and there are other ways to harness energy? Or is it a star map to galaxies we never knew existed? After all, astronomy has always been handed down to our ancestors from 'sky people'. Is it implying that we must seek alternatives to fossil fuels, create more sustainable energy systems and go voyaging among the stars?

Nobody knows if crop circles represent an alien language or a key that opens doors into new civilisations from across our universe. It's a matter of learning to decipher these strange crop circle designs and breaking the code that will open up new knowledge in areas of science and quantum physics.

The Bermuda Triangle – A vortex of doom, a time rip or a portal to other dimensions?

Ships and planes have mysteriously disappeared – vanishing into thin air leaving no wreckage. Planes have faded from radar just as they're about to land. Pilots have radioed hours after their fuel tanks should have been empty, only never to be heard from again. Strange objects in the sky. Compasses malfunctioning. This is the Bermuda Triangle – once known as The Devil's Triangle – a large expanse of the Atlantic Ocean between Florida, Puerto Rico and Bermuda.

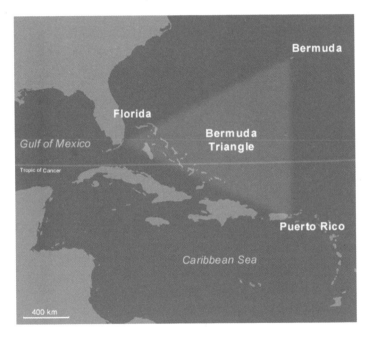

For those who favour the natural explanation, many of the disappearances can be blamed on unique features of this area. The Gulf Stream, a warm ocean current flowing from the Gulf of Mexico around the Florida Straits north-east toward Europe, is very swift and turbulent. There are a number of storms and waterspouts that often spell disaster for ships and planes – this area is known for being in a hurricane path. You also have the huge variation of the ocean floor – from shoals to the deepest trenches in the world. All this flux is ideal for navigational hazards.

Given today's sophisticated navigational technologies, however, should there continue to be mysterious disappearances in this region? The disappearance of Flight 19 still haunts the history books.

Flight 19

On 5 December 1945, five Avenger aircraft set out on a routine training mission to Bimini. They never returned. Two hours after the flight began, the leader of the squadron, Charles Taylor, reported that his compass had become erratic. His back-up compass had failed and his position was unknown. It's common knowledge that a magnetic compass will not point true north in the Bermuda Triangle; it points towards *magnetic* north. This adjustment needs to be made by the navigator. Is this what caused Flight 19 to get lost? Surely the crew were familiar with this flight path and would have made these adjustments and calculations prior to take-off?

After two more hours of confused messages, a distorted radio transmission from the squadron leader was heard saying: 'When the first man gets down to ten gallons of gas, we will land in the water together. Does everyone understand that?'

The last communication took place hours after their fuel supply should have run out. A search plane with a crew of thirteen headed immediately towards Flight 19's last known position. Within twenty minutes of take-off, it too disappeared. No plane. No debris. No wreckage. And no bodies.

Six planes and twenty-seven men – gone. The official report was that stormy weather was responsible for the accident and for not being able to find traces of wreckage. But to this day, Flight 19 remains a tragic victim of the triangle.

It has made people question: Is it a natural phenomenon that needs careful navigation or is the area a gateway to hyperspace – where it is possible to travel at speeds faster than light?

Speculation is that some magnetic forces drag these vessels into a vortex, similar to that of black holes in space. That means that planes and ships could be trapped in wormholes (transit tunnels between different dimensions of reality). It has been suggested that blue holes (small underwater caves, found in this region), might be the transit points for UFOs arriving here from other dimensions.

If other intelligent life is capable of getting here, then there must be ways not only to transcend space-time as we know it, but also to access energy in an abundant way that surpasses the capacity of any energy source currently employed on Earth. It implies that we too could stop using fossil fuels, create more sustainable energy systems and go travelling among the stars.

UFOs and The Bermuda Triangle

In the waters off Andros Island, strange craft that resemble UFOs and display the same astonishing swiftness of motion and sharp turns have been seen from time to time.

Andros Island is the area near the test facility centre, AUTEC CENTRE (Atlantic Undersea Test and Evaluation Centre). Theorists believe that AUTEC might be an underwater Area 51. AUTEC covers only one square mile of land, but the rest is underwater – 1670 square miles (4325 square kilometres). Deep beneath the ocean, it is well away from the public eye.

So many questions remain. Is this region a remnant of the lost continent of Atlantis – a society based on alien technology and information? Is it still a stargate portal for aliens to enter and leave our dimension? Are government agencies aware of UFO activities and are they part of the conspiracy in giving star nations permission to enter? I guess we'll need to wait for the next round of disclosures to solve the Triangle mystery.

Bass Strait Triangle in Australia

We have our own Bermuda Triangle in Bass Strait, between Victoria's mainland and Tasmania. This mysterious triangle encloses a stretch of hostile waters that has claimed ships and planes – some, such as 20-year-old pilot, Frederick Valentich, simply vanishing and never to be found.

Just before radio contact broke down, Valentich reported, 'The thing is just orbiting on top of me.' The communications went dead. Valentich had disappeared into thin air, leaving no trace of oil or metal on land or in sea.

He was flying a single-engine Cessna 182 from Victoria across Bass Strait to King Island on 21 October 1978. His radio report explained the problem he was having: a strange object was hovering above him.

> 'It seems to be playing some sort of game. Flying at a speed I cannot estimate … It has a long shape … green light and sort of metallic light on the outside.'

He also reported seeing a large craft with four bright lights that had caused engine trouble and radio blackout.

Air traffic control attempted to get more details about the aircraft and Valentich cut in on the radio: 'It is hovering and it is not an aircraft.'

Valentich went silent and seconds later there was a metallic sound and radio transmission was cut off. He was never heard from again.

Like the Bermuda Triangle, the Bass Strait Triangle is a dangerous location. It is associated with violent westerly gales and regular movements of the sea floor that in bad weather conditions could create waterspouts or giant waves similar to the vortexes in the Bermuda area.

Valentich's last reported message of a spacecraft hovering over him also confirms the presence of UFOs – just like those that have been witnessed in the area of the Bermuda Triangle. Is it mere coincidence or are these regions a perfect combination of natural forces for UFO contact? Some UFOlogists believe that Valentich did not just disappear, but was abducted by aliens.

Farm Animal Mutilation and UFO Experiments

'...The area was cut away so precisely that there was no way an animal could have done it ... and its body was drained of blood.'

> – *Owner of mutilated male pony, Cisco,*
> *Carmarthen, UK, 29 December 2015*

One of the most bizarre unexplained phenomena has to be farm animal mutilations, where the animal has been butchered with surgical precision. Although this is done mostly to cows, it also happens to horses and sheep. In the US Midwest, thousands of cattle have been lost over the years since 1967 in unexplained or strange circumstances.

Wild predators have been ruled out because of the specific nature of the mutilations. So, if it's not predators and it's not human (no evidence of cults or animal cruelty suspicion), who is responsible for these cruel acts?

These are the puzzling facts: the jaw is cut with precision to expose the jawbone and teeth. The tongue and surrounding glandular tissue have been removed. Other parts removed include sex organs, navel, nipples, anus and glandular tissues. There is no evidence of any blood, despite the serious nature of the injuries The cattle appear to be exsanguinated. Usually the animal is found in the middle of a perfectly created circle. No footprints are noted leading to and from the animal, indicating to some theorists that these animals may have been 'beamed up' to a spacecraft, cut up, then dropped down again.

Why would these organ tissues be so special? It has been suggested that organ tissue retains things picked up in the environment, such as minerals and pesticides. Are cows the most susceptible to these? If the alien theory holds, why is this so important and why cattle? Why not wild mammals that would go undetected by the public?

The cattle mutilations and connection to UFOs was researched by Linda Moulton Howe, who produced a documentary called *A Strange Harvest*. Her work concluded that these mutilations are performed by alien beings who use the animal body parts to test high levels of toxins that humans have put into the atmosphere.

Unmarked government helicopters have been seen in the areas where mutilations took place, used as a ruse to cover up the alien involvement. It seemed to work, as most farmers interviewed about their mutilated stock thought the helicopters meant that the government was doing secret testing in the area.

Mutilations continue to mystify law enforcement agencies and distress farmers. There simply have been no other plausible explanations for this unnecessary animal cruelty.

The 13 Crystal Skulls

Do you believe the number 13 is unlucky? Maybe this unexplained phenomenon will change your mind.

Many people believe that these 13 life-sized crystal skulls with moveable jaws that can reportedly speak or sing are presently scattered all over the world. More importantly, they are due to be reunited. And when they do, it is said that a new era will awaken, which will mean transforming from an old paradigm to a 'new world' – just as the Mayans predicted that 2012 would be the end of the old order.

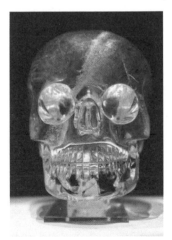

The skulls contain important information about the history of our species on this planet and about our destiny. They were supposedly programmed or encoded by beings from twelve star systems, most of whom have visited Earth before, such as visitors from the Pleiades, Orion, Sirius, Alpha Centauri, Arcturus, Andromeda, Cassiopeia and Zeta Reticuli.

According to Cherokee Native American folklore as retold by Harley Swift-Deer Reagan, the skulls were kept inside a pyramid in a formation of tremendous power known as the Ark. The Ark was made up of the twelve skulls from each of the sacred planets, in a circle, with the thirteenth skull, the largest, placed in the centre of this formation. This thirteenth skull represents the collective consciousness of all the worlds. It connects the knowledge of all the sacred planets.

It is also widely believed that the skulls hold a huge amount of knowledge and each skull contains specialised information – like a living library. Once they are all assembled, the knowledge will be extracted and we can use that knowledge to save our planet.

That's the legend. Now, here's the fact: A real crystal skull was discovered on an archaeological site in Central America in the 1920s by the daughter of English adventurer and traveller, Frederick Mitchell-Hedges. In a lost city in a remote jungle, located in what is now Belize, Central America, Anna Mitchell-Hedges found a perfectly made crystal skull buried beneath an altar in the ruins of a great temple-pyramid.

The crystal skull was more mysterious than anyone could have predicted. Anna Mitchell-Hedges swore that it had healing powers and kept her protected and safe. She felt she could communicate with it telepathically.

Others who saw the skull reported seeing things inside – images, like watching a film. Some even saw past and future events deep inside the crystalline structure.

Many say they have seen a gentle glow, like an aura, extending around the skull, or that they have heard sounds, like the soft chanting of human voices, emanating from it, such that it has now earned the title the 'talking' or 'singing skull'.

Anna Mitchell-Hedges took her skull to one of the world's leading computer companies for rigorous scientific testing. Was it real and from a human and, if so, how old was it?

The scientists were not able to determine the age of the skull – crystal cannot be carbon-dated. However, what surprised them was that the skull and its detachable lower jawbone was made from the same large piece of natural rock crystal.

Even with modern diamond-tipped power tools, the carving process would simply shatter the skull. If it were to be done by hand using only sand and water, it would have taken 300 years! But, to their amazement, there was no evidence of tools having been used at all. One member of the team said, 'This skull shouldn't even exist!'

The skull had been made from the same type of quartz we use in modern electronic equipment. What's unusual about quartz is its ability to control electrical energy and to oscillate at a constant frequency. It sends waves of information – hence the reason quartz crystal is used for electronic equipment such as computers and watches. It is in these devices that information is stored. Are the crystal skulls some kind of information system, as legend suggests?

Native Americans have long believed in the power of quartz crystal. They refer to quartz crystals as 'the brain cells of Mother Earth' and have traditionally used them for healing. There are only 37 known quartz formations and yet there are over 200 types of quartz. It's claimed that the occlusions in the quartz hold the energy, like information programs or energy storage.

Could the skulls be devices to help us communicate with other galaxies and civilisations beyond our world? Native American belief is that the crystal skulls contain information about our own ancestors, about our own past and our own future.

There are several other crystal skulls that claim to be genuine, with powers such as those displayed by the Mitchell-Hedges skull. It's difficult, however, to authenticate them when there are so many copies in the world. Some of the ancient quartz skulls that are believed to be similar to the

Mitchell-Hedges skull are known as Sha Na Ra; ET; Max; Mayan Skull; Einstein; Synergy, and others that are held at the Smithsonian Institution and London and Paris museums.

If the crystal skulls were brought to Earth as gifts from 'the gods', then when all 13 crystals finally come together, there will be great knowledge in how to reconnect with other beings in the galaxy and finally know who we are in the universe.

The Mothman

The *Point Pleasant Register* featured a report with the headline, 'Couples sees Man-Sized Bird ... Creature ... Something'.

The Mothman is a sinister creature who made his terrifying appearance to two young couples from Point Pleasant, West Virginia, in 1966, and was described as 6 to 7 feet (about 2 metres) tall – a 'flying man with ten foot wings' who followed their car. When their car headlights malfunctioned, they were shocked to see a white creature with glowing eyes.

More local people came forward to report their encounters with this terrifying, giant bat-like creature. A farmer's dog was reported to be missing, believed to have been eaten by the Mothman.

It seemed the Mothman had found its perfect home – an abandoned old TNT plant, the site of an old Second World

War munitions plant. The site was heavily forested, with woods, ponds, ridges and hills, tall concrete domes where ammunition was stored, a network of underground tunnels and man-made labyrinths. Most of the area was inaccessible, which made it ideal for the creature to remain undetected.

Many believe that the sightings of the Mothman, together with UFO sightings at the time and encounters afterwards with Men in Black who questioned and intimidated witnesses, are all related. Strange happenings continued in the area for over a year – the most tragic being the collapse of the Silver Bridge on 15 December 1967.

Tragedy and Strange Phenomena

The bridge linking Point Pleasant to Ohio collapsed without warning while it was carrying rush-hour traffic at around 5 pm. Cars plunged into the icy waters of the Ohio River, resulting in 46 deaths. Two of the victims were never found.

On that same evening before the incident, strange lights were reported flashing near the TNT plant and later vanishing into the forest. Author John Keele wrote *The Mothman Prophecies* based on these eerie events around Point Pleasant and the mysterious collapse of the Silver Bridge after UFO sightings.

He began to collect reports for his research, interviewing 100 people who personally witnessed the creature between November 1966 and November 1967. They described the creature as standing between six and seven feet tall, its eyes were set near the top of the shoulders and it had bat-like wings that glided, rather than flapped, when it flew. Witnesses described its skin as being either grey or brown, emitting a humming sound when it flew and, according to a witness, making screeching sounds 'like a woman's scream'.

John Keele also researched other bizarre events in the area, such as issues with television and phone reception, strange lights around the TNT plant, cars stalling without explanation, locked doors that opened and closed by themselves, inexplicable voices, strange sounds and thumps inside and outside people's homes.

Extra-terrestrial or ultra-terrestrial? Does the Mothman belong to a Draconian alien race given that it's a pterodactyloid-like hominoid with bat-like wings? Or is it some sort of dragon creature from Earth? These nocturnal creatures are also known as the Ciakars, Pteroids, Birdmen and Winged Draco and have been encountered near underground systems. In the case of Point Pleasant, was it just coincidence that the bridge collapsed around the time of the Mothman sightings?

Some claimed that the catastrophe was triggered by a sonic boom from the Mothman's wings. Others believed that the Mothman had been sent to warn the people of Point Pleasant of the bridge's imminent collapse, although his message was obviously lost in translation.

Whatever the connection may have been, the Mothman disappeared after the bridge fell down.

Did Tesla Have An ET Connection?

You know Nikola Tesla (1856–1943) because of his ground-breaking inventions – the Tesla coil, alternating current, the induction motor, radio-controlled machines, wireless telegraphy, and a bladeless turbine – to name a few.

He had 278 patents when he died – only he died in debt and his research notes and papers were all auctioned off or stolen after his death. Some say Tesla's files and notes were confiscated by the FBI.

But that's not what makes him so special when it comes to the topic of aliens and UFOs. Tesla was one of the earliest scientists to report that he had communicated with aliens via radio waves.

He claimed he had detected an artificial signal from Mars, or possibly Venus, using high-voltage equipment he had set up at Colorado Springs in 1899. He also predicted that interplanetary communication would 'become the dominating idea of the century that has just begun.'

'I am absolutely certain that they are not caused by anything terrestrial …

The feeling is constantly growing on me that I had been the first to hear the greeting of one planet to another.'

Did Tesla's experiments transmit radio signals to some of our nearer planets or even the moon?

UFOlogists speculate that Tesla was given much alien information about technology, yet controlling governments censored and suppressed his work, inventions and advanced knowledge. Much of Tesla's work remains in the hands of government agencies, and only some of it is just now being understood. Sources say they are being used successfully today in advanced weaponry, including particle-beam weapons, active space travel, time travel, time-warping, anti-gravity devices and more.

What everyone wants to know is, how did Tesla come up with such advanced knowledge? Was it natural genius, did he have an encounter, or did he share some genetics with extra-terrestrials?

Face on Mars

Mars has a face! A human face. That's what we saw in photos taken by NASA's 1976 Viking space probe in the Cydonia region of the planet Mars. More intriguing, the 'face' and other nearby structures have mathematical and geometrical correlations that match those of the Egyptian Sphinx and pyramids.

However, after studying thousands of photos using modern computer technology, the official word from NASA was that it was in fact an optical illusion caused by shadows and older imaging technology – and not a real face at all. It's the pixels' fault we think we see a real face.

That should have been the end of it, but some well-respected scientists, such as one-time NASA consultant Richard Hoagland, disagree. He claims that there is tangible physical evidence of a former civilisation on the planet Mars, one that may be at least 200,000 years old or older. What's more, this civilisation has close connection to the evolution of the human race on Earth.

We now know that there is evidence suggesting Mars was once a wetter, warmer planet, with its northern hemisphere covered in an ocean. Is it not possible, then, that Mars contained intelligent alien life – an ancient civilisation that was more advanced than ours?

Hoagland and his supporters believe that the photos show direct correlation to earthly structures such as the

Sphinx, Stonehenge, Avebury mounds, the Mayan temple ruins, as well as evidence of a fortress, an artificial cliff, a five-sided pyramid and a collection of other spectacular structures – one which he named the 'City Square'. According to Hoagland, it may well date back to a time when, if one stood in the middle of the city square, the summer solstice sun would have risen directly over the 'face'.

The origin of the face still remains a mystery. There are scientists who say that it may be a message from an ancient civilisation beneath the surface of Mars, which may have existed before, or that still exists.

Powerful telescopes from a spacecraft orbiting Mars took pictures of nine pyramids on its surface. The pyramids do not have the characteristics of natural structures. Other images include what appear to be statues of human and animal faces – mostly profiles of primates and canines.

Is it all an optical illusion, as NASA would have us believe?

Could Mars have been a home to a highly developed civilisation before it all ended after a natural catastrophe? There is evidence to suggest that Mars at some stage in its history suffered a catastrophic crustal displacement (slippage of Mars's outer crust). If this took place during the planet's warm and wet phase, any civilisation would have been wiped out in cataclysmic floods and earthquakes. Only scattered ruins and monuments may have been solid enough to survive.

It may even have been the same cataclysm that destroyed Atlantis and created the Great Flood on Earth. Was Mars destroyed completely or did some inhabitants manage to escape, moving to Earth afterwards once the catastrophe had ended?

It would explain the unexplained advancements in our history's timeline. And it would certainly help to explain the connection to the pyramids – especially the Sphinx and the Great Pyramid of Giza. No civilisation on Earth at the time was capable of planning and building such immense engineered structures.

Until NASA sends a manned team to the Cydonia region where the 'face' is, the existence of an alien-created face on Mars is doomed to remain an unexplained phenomenon.

The Starchild Skull

The Starchild Skull is a 900-year-old bone skull, which was found in Mexico in the 1930s. The rest of the skeleton was apparently washed away in a flood. The bizarre skull could not be human, because of some very unusual traits:

- The brain area is 30 per cent larger than normal;
- The skull is lighter but stronger than a human's;

- The inner ear is larger, suggesting the skull is capable of hearing high-frequency sounds;
- The genes of the skull had 56 variations in DNA from that of a human's.

These intriguing results encouraged more research into the ancient skull. The Starchild Project is dedicated to finding the origins of the skull, be it human or alien or a hybrid. The results team ruled out all known deformities; its genetic and physical profile is so different from a human's that it could be a new species.

The Starchild Project has already discovered a high percentage of unusual DNA, and its aim is to recover the entire genome – this will allow experts to determine if the Starchild Skull is indeed a new species. If it's not a human species, the question can only be: 'Then, what is it?'

Stonehenge: The ancient alien theory

Is it a burial site of the elite? An astronomical observatory? A calendar? A Druid temple? An alien landing pad? It's got everyone baffled. Stonehenge on Salisbury Plain, England, is considered the most mysterious prehistoric monument.

This is what we know about Stonehenge: it took 1,500 years to build and is believed to have been constructed around 3000 and 2000 BCE or even earlier.

Its construction is intriguing – it begins with the outer ring, consisting of sarsen sandstone slabs excavated from local quarries in England's Salisbury Plain; the inner ring is built with bluestone rocks that are believed to be from Preseli Hills in Wales, nearly 200 miles (322 kilometres) away.

How could the ancient people have transported huge boulders weighing over 4 tons (3.6 tonnes) over such vast distances with primitive Neolithic transport and instruments? This is the exact question that is posed about the construction of the Great Pyramid of Giza.

Who was responsible for this feat if not humans? Did aliens with their superior knowledge of technology and engineering come to our aid?

Erich von Däniken claims that Stonehenge was a model of our solar system, serving both the solar and lunar calendar. The line betwcen the Heel Stone and the Altar Stone extends to the precise point of midsummer sunrise. This visual information was not only for the benefit of humans, who gained knowledge of astronomy, but the stone circle served as both a landing pad for spaceships and as an astronomical observatory for the heavens as well as UFOs.

Are UFOlogists closer to the truth in saying that it was alien-assisted, them giving us a helping hand and guiding us to advance our technological development? Or if we are to take the ancient Sumerian texts literally, like the Anunnaki, that the aliens may have had their own agenda? Visits were not simply space voyages for exploration, but for potential genetic experimentation and mineral extractions.

On another note, Stonehenge and other ancient megaliths, such as the Rollright Stones in Oxfordshire, were said to have healing properties. They are believed to exhibit rapid fluctuations of magnetic energy and for centuries the locals believed that if a person suffered from bone fractures, a visit to the Stones would mend them. It's interesting that modern medicine endorses that electromagnetism does indeed accelerate the healing process.

Was this something ancient people figured out for themselves, or did it need superior alien knowledge?

Ley (energy) Lines

You can't see ley lines. They are invisible to human eyes. You can, however, feel them.

Imagine invisible intersecting energy lines that crisscross the entire planet. They are created through cracks in the tectonic plate, where the natural energy is released, and are thought to have spiritual and healing properties. More significantly, they are connected with ancient mysterious structures, UFO sightings and alien visitations.

English researcher Alfred Watkins noticed that ancient monuments such as standing stones, burial mounds and significant sites fell into straight lines with each other or at exact angles, even when displaced for miles. In 1921, he named these energy paths ley lines.

Ancient civilisations have known about ley lines or energy paths forever. Most sacred monuments were built upon them, designed to harness natural power and energy from the Earth.

Some of the greatest ancient monuments are connected by the grid of ley lines – Stonehenge, Macchu Pichu, the Great Pyramid of Giza, the Easter Island sculptures, the Sphinx, and other natural rock formations such as Uluru in Central Australia.

It's widely questioned whether the mysterious Great Pyramid of Giza was in fact a geo-magnetic power plant that converted the energy of the ley lines or energy paths from the Earth into electricity. One of the most puzzling artefacts is an ancient Egyptian carving of what looks like an electric light bulb.

Australian Aboriginals, who are strongly connected to the land and feel the energy of the ley lines as electromagnetic fields, believe that the land is alive and it sings songs celebrating the life and creation of Mother Earth.

Native American Indians call ley lines 'spirit lines'. Shamans used the electromagnetic energy from ley lines to design their medicine wheels. The Druids called ley lines 'mystical lines', the Welsh called them 'dragon lines'. In China they are known as *lung-mei* or 'dragon paths'. This is closely linked with the concept of energy meridians that are connected to acupuncture.

Interestingly, there seems to be a boost of electromagnetic energy when two or more ley lines intersect. This creates a power point and an energy force.

Ley lines and UFOs

Many UFO sightings have been witnessed near or upon ley lines. How are they connected? It's widely assumed that UFOs tap into the electromagnetic field for energy. People claim to have seen UFOs hovering between mobile-phone towers and at aluminium smelters.

Another theory is that they may use ley lines as points of navigation, much like wormholes in space-time travel.

Many crop circles have also appeared near or on top of ley lines. Are they related? Do these energy points attract extra-terrestrial visitors? Is it a coincidence that crop circles in England are also located near ancient sacred sites such as Stonehenge, Avebury and Silbury Hill?

It seems obvious that ancient civilisations and extra-terrestrials understand the power of energy and ley lines – it may take us a little longer to work it out.

The truth Is Still Out There

John Podesta has been US President Barack Obama's transition leader and close adviser. He also served as Bill Clinton's Chief of Staff. He is now the chairman of Hillary Clinton's presidential campaign.

His famous tweet on 13 February 2015 made world news: 'Finally, my biggest failure of 2014: Once again not securing the disclosure of the UFO files.'

He believes that there are classified files that need to be released and he is disappointed that he has not been able to expose the truth about UFOs to the American people.

'The time to pull the curtain back on this subject is long overdue … it is definitely time for government, scientists, and aviation experts to work together in unravelling the questions about UFOs that have so far remained in the dark.'

With so many prominent astronauts, scientists, politicians, military personnel and eminent people all disclosing that they have witnessed UFOs, it's no longer the time to ask ourselves, 'Are we alone?' It's more likely to be, 'We have never been alone.' Our ancestors spoke of gods from heaven seeding our planet and giving us information way beyond our capabilities at the time. Time and time again we've seen and heard evidence – whether it's through art, stories, texts, photography, movies or hypnosis – and yet most of us don't want to believe that there is intelligent life in our universe and beyond other than our own.

Our government agencies have covered up the truth about a number of unexplained UFO phenomena and have admitted to doing so. It was done for the public good, apparently; to avoid mass panic. This may have been the case in the 1940s, but today it's another generation altogether.

Throughout Earth's history, in all cultures, beliefs and religions, governments have had confidential and secret treatises for the benefit of a small number of people on the planet. Most known alien contact has been positive, however the negative spin has created fear and cover-ups. Some believe that governments agreed to aliens testing human–alien genetic modifications as long as they were minimal and documented. This did not always happen, as is evident from horrifying abduction stories, mutilations and excessive testing.

The technological and scientific era has meant that we are much more aware of our capabilities and our place in the universe. There has never been more at stake to protect our planet, with global warming and the potential destruction of our environment.

There is a shared belief that extra-terrestrial beings are here, now, because we are at a crucial point in evolution. More than ever, we need help to get through this period in time when the future of our environment is under extreme threat. If indigenous prophecies are correct, we are due for an increase in frequency and intensity of planetary changes – most of which could negatively impact Mother Earth.

More than ever we need some guidance to keep us from destroying our Earth and each other.

If there are any extra-terrestrials out there paying attention, now would be a good time to share some new knowledge that will help humanity shift towards a new way of living – as the Hopi predicted – the beginning of the fifth world.

References/Bibliography

Books

Blumrich, Josef, *The Spaceships of Ezekiel,* New York: Bantam 1974

Keele, John, *The Mothman Prophecies*, New York: Tor Books 2002

Churchward, James, *The Lost Continent of Mu*, Brotherhood of Life 1987

von Däniken, Erich, *Chariots of the Gods,* New York: Berkeley Books 1977

Sitchin, Zecharia, *The Lost Book of Enki*, Vermont: Bear and Company 2002

Mitchell, Edgar, D., *The Way of the Explorer: An Apollo Astronaut's Journey Through the Material and Mystical Worlds*, New Jersey: The Career Press 2008

Bainton, Roy, *The Mammoth Book of Unexplained Phenomena*, London: Constable & Robinson Ltd 2013

Shuker, Karl, P.N., *The Unexplained: An Illustrated Guide to the World's Natural and Paranormal Mysteries*, Carlton Books Ltd 1996

Waters, Frank, *The Book of the Hopi*, Penguin Books 1963

Hoagland, Richard C., *The Monuments of Mars: A City on the Edge of Forever* (5th ed.), Berkeley: Frog, Ltd. 2002

Magazines
New Dawn Magazine
National Geographic

Websites
http://www.disclosureproject.org/
(Dr Steven Greer)
http://www.auforn.com/
(Australian UFO research centre)
https://vault.fbi.gov/Roswell%20UFO
(FBI files on Roswell sighting)
http://www.archives.gov/research/military/air-force/ufos.html
(national archives military records)
http://www.educatinghumanity.com/
    2012/03/ufo-theory-sightings-research-reports.html -
    sthash.LPzYzAWe.dpuf
(UFO conspiracy theories)

About the Author

Rose is one of Australia's most popular dream researcher, author and presenter. She presents seminars, workshops and courses in Australia and overseas, with frequent media appearances on radio, television and magazines. She has helped a number of clients interpret their dreams in her capacity of dream group facilitator and is a member of the International Association for the Study of Dreams.

Her first book on dreams, *Dictionary of Dreams*, is an international best seller. Following on from this success, *Dreams – What Your Subconscious Wants to Tell You* and *Dream Reading Cards* are proving to be very popular in both mainstream and Mind Body Spirit genre.

Rose has spent the last 25 years writing children's books and is a successfully published children's author of over 60 books. She has been listed in the Notable Children's Books and short-listed for the Environment Award for Children's Literature in Australia.

Her love of researching into mysterious phenomena began in her teaching days, when she strived to inspire her students to delve further into the mysteries of the universe, using information from science and myth to form an educated opinion. There seems to be no adequate explanation for the unexplained events on our planet and when it comes to UFOs and aliens, Rose has interviewed those who have witnessed sightings that authorities have no record of.

As the world is more open to the possibility that we are not alone on this planet, projects to uncover information previously withheld from the public, such as the Disclosure Project, have created an unprecedented interest to find out more.

As a global citizen, Rose's dream is to be self sufficient and live off the grid on the land. She has started this process on her farm in country Victoria where she grows olive trees and harvests organic olives for the purest olive oil. The property has a clear night sky, where it is possible to catch a glimpse of a UFO or two.